Creating

Effective
Spaces

Creating Effective Spaces

How to Declutter, Organize, and Maintain Your Space

Contents

Getting personal

If you follow me on social media, you will know that I don't reveal much about my personal life. I prefer to share ideas about how I create effective spaces for myself and others—ideas that can also help you. I think it is important to keep some personal things to yourself, so I'll be brief here.

I grew up in the UK and worked in sales for most of my career. I then moved to Australia in 2004, where I now live with my partner, Gavin, two beautiful but messy boys, Joey and Benji, and our Labrador, Archie. Gavin is Irish, and I flew to the other side of the world to meet him. That is very typical of me!

In 2018, Gavin and I were over the moon to welcome our first child, Joey, into the world. At the local mothers' group, I met many beautiful people. But I don't think Effective Spaces would be what it is today without one person in particular: Krystal, thank you.

Before I met Krystal, I was unaware that organizing, or more specifically helping other people organize their homes, could be a career path. I had spent years organizing my own spaces, and those of family and friends, but I had never considered generating income from it (more fool me).

One day in 2019, Krystal questioned why I wasn't earning a living from organizing spaces, and that was it: my light bulb moment. You could say the rest is history, but there is a little more.

Our second child, Benji, was due in January 2020, and although I knew at this point that I wanted to set up my own business, I was also aware it would be a challenge.

"I share ideas about how I create effective spaces for myself and others"

Joey was only one, Gavin and I were both working full time, and all our family lived overseas. I had my hands full. On the flip side, running my own business would mean I could control the hours I worked, and hence the hours I spent with my babies. Having organized countless spaces, I knew I could do it well and knew the impact I could make. With Gavin's full support, I took the plunge and resigned from my full-time role. I built a very bad website, set up my social media accounts, and started sharing content.

We all know what happened next: COVID-19. Three months after setting up my business, hustling to get clients (paying clients, finally), and giving birth to Benji, we were in lockdown. Ultimately, my brand new, rapidly growing business was forced to come to a halt—for quite some time. I was unable to go into other people's homes, I had two growing boys to feed, and I had bills to pay. So, I reached out to my former employer in the hope they had some work. Thankfully, they did, and I fully appreciate how lucky I was to be able to return to work.

As my social media accounts had already started to gain momentum, and we were all unsure what the impact of COVID-19 would be, I wanted to keep sharing my knowledge online. I was replying to specific requests about folding, organizing, and gift wrapping. Most of my filming was done during the early mornings—often at 2, 3, even 4 a.m. It was the only time I had. Looking back, I don't know how I made it work, but I am so glad I did.

And here we are now, a global community, and not much has changed for me. I spend most of my time with my boys, I still work part time in the corporate sector, and I share my knowledge online. My videos are still too fast (yes, I read your comments), but I enjoy what I do.

I also believe that giving back to others is one of the greatest privileges we have in life, so I will continue to fulfil requests on my social media (@effectivespaces) for folding, organizing, and gift wrapping. I certainly never expected millions of people would enjoy what I share. But, together, we have built a community of more than 10 million people. How does that even make sense?

Naturally, I am very aware that what I share is nothing extraordinary: I fold, I organize, and I wrap gifts. I do not give back to others in the sense of saving lives, but I always try to do my bit: working to my strengths and making an impact that way.

I am grateful for the thousands of images, messages, emails, and videos I receive from our community. To be welcomed into so many homes across the world is an honor, and one I will never take for granted.

For this, I thank you.

xx

My home

My home is not perfect, and I wouldn't want it to be. I certainly don't have the most aesthetically pleasing space, as you can see on my social media. When I first started sharing content, I was conscious that my home is not the stereotypical beige and white open-plan space that appears all over your "For You" page: all clean lines, fancy flooring, and marble countertops.

If you look under my posts, it is easy to find comments such as, "That's so old," "Your shelves need a coat of paint," and "Yuck." Comments like these only hold merit if such things are important to you, and it didn't take me long to realize that for me they are not.

Social media can be a brutal place at times, but it can also be somewhere you find kindness, love, and support from like-minded people who see past the chipped paintwork. They are my kind of people.

So, I am not ashamed to show my home, flaws and all. It is filled with everything that is important to me, and I feel very fortunate. Some people are able to change their spaces physically, whereas others are more limited in what they can do—here's to the renters, like me! We are all unique. That is why, when it comes to organizing, what works for one person may not work for another.

With that in mind, what we are going to cover—and what I hope you will achieve by the end of this book—is how to organize to suit your own personal needs. Please remember that organizing is a skill and it takes time and energy. Take your time, have some fun, and enjoy the process.

"I am not afraid to show my home, flaws and all."

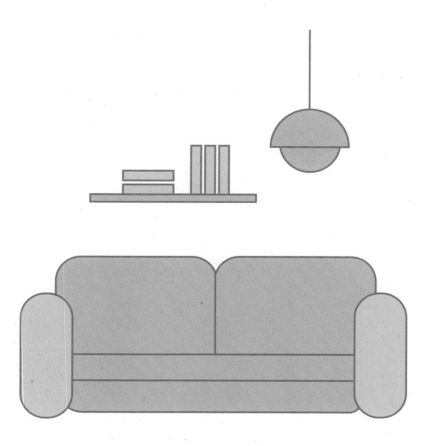

The Basics

Some people are naturally more organized than others. Please don't let that deter you. Organizational skills can be learned and developed. The more you practice, the easier it becomes. Let's start with the basics and take a look at some of my fundamental principles that can help you create an effective space.

What is an effective space?

The purpose of having effective spaces is the same in all homes. Effective spaces save you time and money. They reduce stress and anxiety, and enable you to be more in control of your environment. What an effective space looks like is subjective, though, because it is governed by individual needs. Not mine, not your friends', and certainly not those you see on social media. Your space has to be about you.

To establish what your personal needs are, we have to figure out what is happening in your spaces and what is essential to you in and around your home. Then, we can start organizing your items so your essentials are easy to see, access, and put back. This will make your effective space much easier to maintain.

Before we begin, we have to agree on one thing: we are not here to create perfectly curated spaces. Contrary to what we see on social media, making a space look good only plays a key role in organizing if aesthetics are all-important to you personally. I have worked with many clients for whom the aesthetic of their space is not a priority. Does this mean they are disorganized and do not have an effective space? No. For them, it is more important that the space functions well, saves them time, and is easy to take care of.

So, I will never advise you to buy lots of jars and bottles for your kitchen just so you can decant food that is already in perfectly adequate packaging. Your space might look amazing once you have arranged your containers, but—reality check—who is going to wash and dry them every week or so? Not me. Anything that is time-consuming to maintain is not practical; it is not what organizing effectively is about.

There is a sweet spot where functionality, maintenance, and form meet, but we have to get the first two right in order for the third to be sustainable. This is why we create effective spaces that suit our own needs, not someone else's. Fortunately, no matter the size or shape of your space, or what your priorities may be, I have some fundamental principles that will help you on your journey to organizing successfully.

Function before form, with ease of maintenance the primary goal

Small space, big impact

Always start small. I'm sure you have heard this before, but let's take it one step further. There is no point starting small if you do not feel the impact of your newly organized space immediately. So, choose a space that is small in size, but one that will make a big difference once it is organized.

I suggest a high-traffic area. If you feel the benefits of your efforts every day, you will be motivated to continue your organizing journey. If you start with a space that is rarely used, you will not get enough satisfaction. You may experience a quick burst of pride when you realize how well the space works and how easy things are to find and put away, but we need to go bigger than that. Not in terms of space, but in terms of benefit.

Where to start

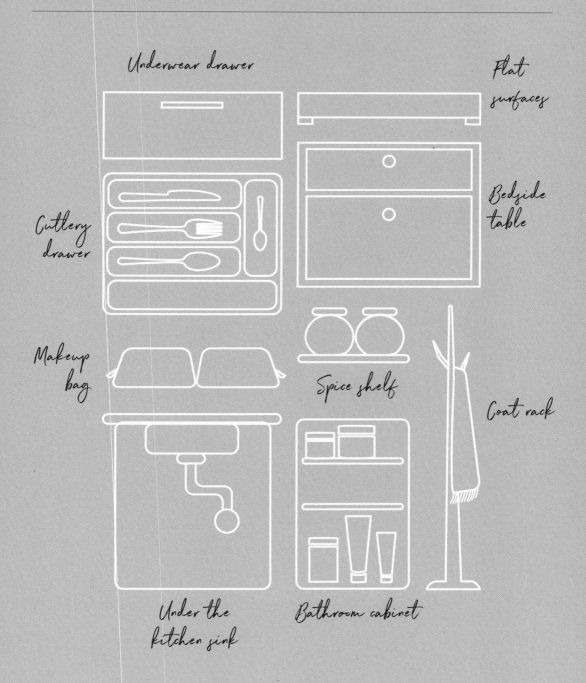

Underwear drawer

Flat surfaces

Cutlery drawer

Bedside table

Makeup bag

Spice shelf

Coat rack

Under the kitchen sink

Bathroom cabinet

Keep things close to where you use them

This concept is simple but game-changing. The closer items are to where you use them, the more efficient your day will be.

For example, at our house, the dog's leash hangs on a hook outside the front door. That is where we attach the leash before we go for a walk, so it is exactly where it needs to be. The umbrella is on a hook beside the leash.

This means that Archie (our dog) doesn't have to wait—overexcited—while I traipse through the house looking for his leash. And then wait again when I realize I have forgotten the umbrella. You get the idea! This routine might raise my step count, but the moral of the story is: store things where you use them, or as close as they can be, because it will save you time.

Think before you buy containers

I know how exciting it is to start your organizing journey, to take inspiration from various social media pages and the thousands of beautiful images on Pinterest. And I understand you might want to rush out and buy an assortment of jars, baskets, and stackable containers to get your home organized immediately. Please don't. Take your time to decide what you really need, and read product reviews. There are a lot of items on the market, and quality can be questionable. As the old saying goes: "Buy well; buy once." If you have to wait to source something that is better quality, then wait. It will save you money in the long run.

When you have decided which containers you need, keep the theme consistent (same color/material). You don't want a mix of styles, because it will make your space look disjointed.

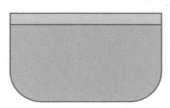

Forget the complex systems

Decanting every item in your pantry, having 30 containers in your refrigerator, and sorting LEGO by color—I appreciate the aesthetics of complex systems, but who has the time to maintain them? We really don't need to overcomplicate things and waste time cleaning containers or sorting unnecessarily. Organizing is about saving time so you can do more of the things you love.

As a working mom, the last thing on my mind is to make sure that our LEGO is sorted by color. How do I organize LEGO? For younger children, I find that a drawstring bag works perfectly well to simply keep the LEGO all in one place. For others, I sort by type, and we go from there. It may take a little time, but this system means that the different LEGO pieces are easy to find when building.

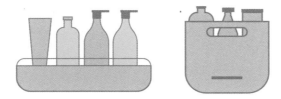

Less is more

Hands up if you get entranced by restocking videos on social media. I, too, have watched them for longer than I care to admit. As entertaining as they are, I have an issue with some of them, and it's quite a big one. Why is it that so many spaces are completely full? They are crammed with products. It's as if a space needs to be full in order for it to look better, and I really struggle with this concept.

I acknowledge that some people like wearing makeup and will have a lot of it. Some people love shoes and will have more than I would wear in a lifetime. For me, it's books. But I wouldn't go out and buy more books just to fill a space. If a space isn't full, it doesn't mean it isn't effective—quite the opposite. So, please, if there are empty spaces in your drawers or cupboards, or on your shelves, leave them alone. Give your items space to breathe and yourself room to grow.

"If a space isn't full, it doesn't mean it isn't effective."

Label in broad categories

Labels play an important role in the organizing process. They are the equivalent of an address, directing everyone to where an item lives. Thus, they are your ticket to maintaining an organized space.

Labels are also a great way for children to learn. They can help with spelling and can encourage children to participate in tidying up. I often get comments on social media when people see that I have labeled our pasta jar. It is a clear container, and of course I can identify pasta without a label, but labeling is a simple way to incorporate learning into everyday life.

I also have to mention here the importance of getting labeling right. Keep your categories broad. The more specific the label, the more complex the system, and the more time it will take to maintain. Let's use the bathroom as an example. Broad categories for labels would be "hair," "face," "body." More specific categories would be "hair accessories," "shampoo," "styling products." At the start of your organizing journey, I suggest you have one container labeled "hair" to house your shampoo, styling products, and so on. Within that same container, you would also store hair accessories. Because some accessories tend to be quite small, place them in their own jar so they are easy to access and return.

Establishing what is essential to you will impact your labeling. I recently organized a chef's home, and the pantry was, understandably, huge. We decanted and labeled about 20 items, which is in stark contrast to the 6 I decant in my own pantry. My client needs to be able to see stock levels at a glance, which you can do when you store items in clear containers. Categories were specific due to the nature of his work. In comparison, his bathroom has five containers, with broadly labeled categories.

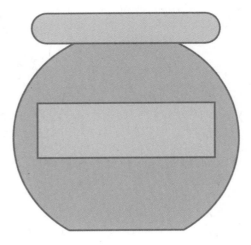

Set boundaries

Your home will naturally set boundaries for you. There are ways to create more space in a kitchen cabinet (see page 154) but, without remodeling your kitchen, there is a limit to what you can do. Boundaries will, therefore, be different depending on your lifestyle and the size of your space. What remains the same, however, is that if you ignore the boundaries, things will creep out of control.

Let's imagine you have a dedicated drawer for sportswear that is already full, and there is a sale at your favorite sportswear shop. Without decluttering, you are going to exceed your boundary because your sportswear drawer isn't miraculously going to double in size. If you put your new items in a different drawer, what happens when you go to find them? Can you remember where you put them because your sportswear drawer was full? Did you actually put them away, or are they still in their bag at the back of your closet?

When organizing your items, the containers you choose will help set your boundaries. If your storage box for bed linen is full, for example, it probably means you do not need any more bed linen. If you buy new sets, get rid of some old ones to make room for them. Don't just store the new bedding elsewhere. Let the containers guide you. Remember: respect your boundaries.

SET BOUNDARIES

Fold to save time

There is a common misconception that my folding methods are designed to make items smaller so you can fit more into a space. I am here to debunk that myth.

All my folding techniques are designed to save you time. Some items may end up smaller than if you folded them in the traditional manner, but that is a bonus. It is not the main reason why I fold the way I do.

No one, myself included, wants to refold items that have already been folded. It's a waste of time, and it's unnecessary. I fold in such a way that I don't have to refold anything. When I take a T-shirt from the drawer, for example, all the other T-shirts remain intact, even if they fall over. The folds do not unravel. My methods are working smarter not harder.

Importantly, my folds are childproof, or as close to childproof as something can be. Children love to rummage around in drawers, and you can add childproof locks if you like, but where is the fun in that? Just make sure your items are folded so they stay folded. Then everybody wins.

Avoid stacking clothes in piles

There are very few items that I store in piles, because piles are not easy to maintain. Think about clothing stores, where there are often piles of clothes on display. Having worked in retail, I have spent many hours putting together such displays. But I have spent many more hours maintaining them because as soon as someone pulls out their size, other items are dislodged. The same applies at home. If you have to lift up one item to reach another, your pile will become messy. Of course, you can rearrange it each time, but you don't have to store things in piles. There are better ways to create effective spaces that are much easier to maintain.

Let's use a bookstore as an example. Books that are piled up on the central display are always identical: same title, same author. But the books in the rest of the store are arranged vertically, in horizontal rows. They are easy to see, remove, and replace. Storing items in this way at home makes far more sense.

When we pile up items, the ones at the bottom are harder to reach. There is, therefore, a tendency to select those that are close to the top. Let me ask you: if you store your clothes in piles, when was the last time you wore the item at the bottom of the pile? And if you stored your clothing in a row, would you wear more of your items because you can reach them all easily?

There are always exceptions, so here are a few tips if you still want to store your items in piles or on shelves:

- Fold items as flat as possible to prevent the pile from toppling over.

- Ensure only one crease is showing. This will stop you picking up multiple items at the same time and messing up the pile.

- Three is the magic number. The more items in your pile, the harder it will be to reach the ones toward the bottom.

Tops

1. Start with the sweater flat and face down.

2. Fold each sleeve over, until the cuff lines up with the opposite side of the collar.

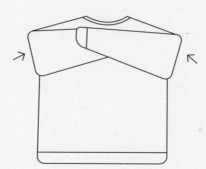

3. Fold each side of the sweater into the center until they meet.

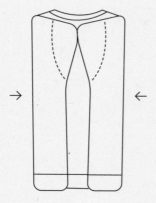

4. Fold the top of the sweater down.

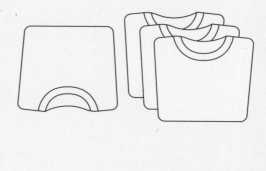

Towels

1. Fold the towel in half. Leave a gap where the edges meet.

2. Fold in half again.

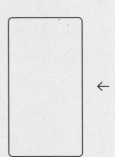

3. If you store your towels on deep shelves, fold up from the bottom once.

4. For narrower shelves, fold up from the bottom twice.

FOLD TO SAVE TIME

Jeans

1. Start with the jeans flat and the zipper facing up. Fold each leg from the bottom to the top, leaving a gap.

2. Repeat the fold from the bottom to the top, again leaving a gap.

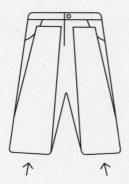

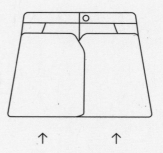

3. Fold the jeans over from left to right, and ensure the label is showing, so you can identify each pair.

4. Store in a pile with one seam facing out, so when you take a pair, you are only picking up one at a time.

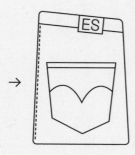

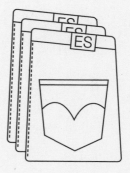

When organizing your cabinets and closets, make sure you only need to open one door to access the item you want. Treat the center section as a boundary.

Hidden gems

This is one for people taking care of children. My organizing techniques are designed so you only need to use one hand. Storing items vertically, in a horizontal row, means that you can pick up something with one hand, without messing up the drawer or shelf. Like the pile of clothes at the clothing store, the more you have to touch other items to reach what you want, the messier the pile becomes.

Decluttering

Many of us dive right into the decluttering and organizing processes without any forethought. We must look at the bigger picture first.

The main objective is to design functional spaces that suit our specific requirements. So, make yourself a cup of tea, or pour a glass of wine, and let's begin.

Assess
your home

I always ask these three questions before organizing any space, whether it's in my own home or in someone else's. They help peel back the layers, find out what is going on in the space, and establish what is important.

1	*2*	*3*
What is working?	What is not working?	What items are essential?

" There will be something you already do that is working."

Q1: What is working?

"Nothing. Everything is a mess. I hate it." This is a common response to this question. But there is always *something* that is working, so let's look more closely.

Do you put your wallet and keys in a specific place? Are your cleaning products stored together in one cabinet? Is there a certain spot where you keep the dog's leash? Are your belts arranged so you can see them all?

With all the noise on social media and numerous programs on TV about decluttering and organizing, it is easy to forget that you already have the foundations in place for creating your own organizing systems. Almost certainly, there will be something you already do that is working for you. You just have to take a moment to find it.

By taking a good look at what you like about your home, and which spaces are easy to maintain, you can replicate these systems in other areas.

Q2: What is not working?

This is your time to whine and complain. Go ahead; let it all out. The areas we recognize as "not working" are the ones we need to focus on. Be thorough and precise, because little things can slip through the cracks. For example, here are some responses from one client:

"I am sick of losing my car keys and spending 10 minutes every morning searching for them. Then, I'm late taking the kids to school."

"I can never find my phone, wallet, or glasses."

"I'm tired of falling over the kids' shoes, bags, and coats that are thrown by the door."

"I really don't like being in my home office. It makes me feel on edge because it is used as a dumping ground. I cannot work efficiently there."

"Items get lost in the back of my cupboards, so I waste a lot of money buying things I already have."

"I have nowhere to store gift wrap, the vacuum, and my spare duvet."

Over to you. Write down as many things as you like. Keep your list safe, stick it on the refrigerator, and then you can work through them, one by one.

Q3: What items are essential?

I am not going to suggest you throw everything out (breathe a sigh of relief). A more effective way to organize is to identify what is essential to you within a space. When we take the time to establish which items we use in a particular space, we are identifying not only those that need to stay where they are but also those that don't. We are, therefore, subconsciously creating an action plan. This will be helpful for Step 1 of the decluttering process (see page 41), during which you will decide what to do with your nonessential items.

Your motivation

Ask yourself those three questions each time you organize a space, big or small. Following this process takes the onus away from purging and focuses your thoughts on how to create an effective space.

But before we roll up our sleeves and get started, I must ask: Why do you want to get organized?

- Is it to save money, because it will stop you buying things you already have?

- Is it because you want to be more efficient?

- Is it so you can relax at home?

Whatever your reason, use it as your motivation. Whenever you are feeling overwhelmed by the task ahead, remind yourself why you want to get organized, turn up the music, and keep going.

Streamline your space

The reality is, everything we do is much harder if a space is cluttered. If your kitchen is in disarray, it makes cooking, cleaning, and food preparation more difficult because you have to navigate your way around other items to find or do what you need.

If you want to get organized and create effective spaces that serve you better, you need to declutter first. Here are three steps to help you:

1	*2*	*3*
Clear and edit the space: Edit as you go and clear the space entirely.	Create categories: Sort items into piles, like with like.	Reassess: Take another look at the items you have left.

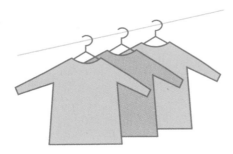

Decluttering may seem like a formidable task, but it is critical if you want spaces that are functional, stress free, and easy to maintain. My three-step decluttering process will allow you to:

- Maximize space by removing unnecessary and unwanted items

- Simplify the organizing process

- Identify what is essential and what is not

- Reduce stress by creating a calmer, more manageable environment

- Save time and energy in the long run

Before you start to declutter, make sure you have asked yourself "What is working?," "What is not working?," and "What items are essential?" in relation to your space. If you decide something is essential, then keep it. But do your childhood ballet trophies, for example, need to occupy prime real estate, or could they be stored elsewhere? Here are a few alternative storage options for sentimental items:

- Attic

- Basement

- Corner space

- Top cabinet

- Any area that is hard to reach or that you don't use frequently

Now, put on some comfy clothes, and let's begin. Check that you have boxes and trash bags ready, find a notepad so you can list any items that have passed their expiration date and need to be replaced, and get out your cleaning materials.

Step 1: Clear and edit the space

Have a bag or box for each of the following categories: "throw away," "pass on," and "store." You can lay out in front of you all the items you want to "keep" in the space.

We want the area we are working on to be completely empty at the end of Step 1, and by "empty" I mean nothing left at the back of any drawers, shelves, or cabinets. Focus on what is important to you within the space, and prioritize items that you use frequently rather than items you might use someday. If you have already answered the question "What items are essential?," this process will be far simpler. For some items, the decision may not be easy. If you need further assistance in the decision-making process, please refer to the Q&A section (see page 48).

Edit as you go. Take items out one by one, and make a decision then and there. If you pick up something and know it will end up in the "pass on" box, put it there right away. The same goes for things that need to be thrown away. Another reason to edit as you go is to avoid decision fatigue, because this can impair your ability to make effective choices. I recommend doing little and often.

For essential items you want to keep, start to create categories (see Step 2). Where possible, we want to avoid wasting time and sorting items more than once.

After everything has been cleared, give the space a thorough clean.

Your go-to guide

Keep

Items that are essential and serve a purpose in day-to-day life.

Pass on

Items that might be useful to someone else. There are a few options as to what you can do with things in this category. You could donate, sell, or recycle them, or you could pass them on to a friend.

Childcare facilities and preschools are often looking for materials they can use for art and craft activities, or you could post your items on a local online marketplace. Whatever you decide, store your "pass on" items outside the house, so they don't creep back into your newly organized space.

Throw away

Items beyond repair, that have expired, and that people wouldn't purchase secondhand.

Store

Seasonal and sentimental items. Grab some storage containers, label them, and stack them neatly in a designated area (attic, basement, garage).

Step 2: Create categories

Step 2 is really a continuation of Step 1. If you edited while clearing out in Step 1, you will already have created some categories for items you want to keep. Now you need to sort the rest of your essential items. Keep your categories as broad as possible: jeans, tops, shorts, or spices, dried food, canned food. Avoid complex systems; they are both confusing and time consuming. And remember: the way in which you categorize your items only has to make sense to you.

Having completed the first two steps, you will have the items you wish to keep laid out in front of you in their natural groupings.

Step 3: Reassess

It's now time to take one last look. Reassessing your categorized items gives you another chance to spot any double- or triple-ups you may have missed. Do you really need three whisks, for example? Take a good look at what you have decided to keep, and discard more items if you need to.

STREAMLINE YOUR SPACE

Regret-free decluttering

It is common to experience a feeling of guilt when you are decluttering, so let's address that right now.

Some items may have sentimental value, and by all means store these elsewhere. Other items may have monetary value. If an item was expensive, and you feel guilty about how much it cost, you are projecting even more value on to the item. Is it essential you keep it just because it was expensive, or could someone else use the item and get value from it? If you are keeping an item but not using it, then it has no true value to you anyway.

The prospect of decluttering your home can be daunting, and you may worry that you will regret some of your decisions. No need! I've put together a list of 20 items that you can confidently purge from your home with no regrets. It's a great way to make progress.

For more guidance, follow my 28-day decluttering challenge on pp.46–47.

1. Mismatched socks

2. Dried-up or unusable craft supplies

3. Old bed linen (donate to local animal shelter)

4. Broken toys/games and puzzles

5. Old calendars/diaries

6. Clothes with holes (unless you can darn)

7. Dead batteries

8. Expired makeup

9. Old magazines

10. Herbs and spices you have never used

11. Unused recipe books

12. Old menus

13. Food storage containers that don't have lids

14. Expired medication (drop off at a dedicated local take-back site)

15. Old receipts (unless they are guarantees or you need them for accounting purposes)

16. Shoes that hurt

17. Old towels and blankets

18. Chipped or cracked mugs/dishes

19. Laptops, phones, and chargers that are no longer used

20. Expired condiments

1

2

3

4

5

6

7

8

9

10

11

12

13

14

15

16

17

18

19

20

STREAMLINE YOUR SPACE

28-day decluttering

Week 1

- Cutlery drawer
- Spices
- Mugs and cups
- Refrigerator
- Kitchen counters
- Cleaning supplies
- Junk drawer

Week 2

- Car
- Flat surfaces in bedrooms and living space
- Bathroom cabinet
- TV stand/sideboard
- Hallway
- Linen closet
- Handbags or work bags

Week 3

- Kids' school bags
- Kids' books and games
- Toys
- Makeup
- Hair accessories and jewelery
- Wallets and occasional bags
- Bedside tables

Week 4

- Underwear drawer(s)
- Activewear and swimwear
- Shoes
- Jeans and tops
- Sunglasses, hats, and scarves
- Finish any areas from weeks 1 to 3
- Celebrate your progress!

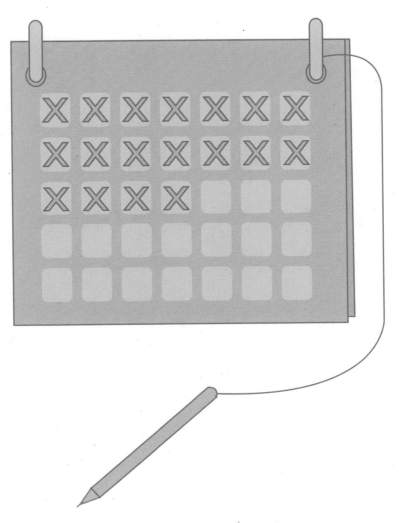

As you work through your decluttering plan, remind yourself of all the positive aspects of the process. It will free up space for things that are essential. It will save you time, because you won't have to search through clutter to find something. It will save you money, because you won't buy items that you already have but can't find. It will make you feel more in control. A space without clutter will also boost your mood, help promote relaxation, and provide clarity. The benefits are endless.

STREAMLINE YOUR SPACE

Q&A

"I don't know what to get rid of. Please help."

Hopefully, reading this chapter will already have helped answer this question. Ultimately, you have to decide which items are essential to you within your space. If something is not serving a purpose, and is simply taking up valuable space, then it is time for it to go. Additional questions to ask yourself include:

- When was the last time I used it? (This excludes seasonal items—I love our Christmas mugs.)

- Do I like it? You might like something but never use it. If this is the case, keep it but don't let it take up valuable real estate. If you don't like it but use it, ask yourself how often you need to use it.

- Does this item add value? If not, can I let it go without regretting it?

- Is it sentimental? If an item is sentimental, ask yourself *how* sentimental it is. Can it be donated so someone else can enjoy it, or should it be stored elsewhere?

Remember: you will not lose part of yourself by letting an item go. Objects do not define who you are. You don't always need a physical reminder because you have your memories.

Q&A

"My partner struggles to part with things, what can I do?"

I can relate to this very well because Gavin is similar. It would be great if you could persuade your partner to read this book, but I'm guessing that won't happen. A few suggestions that have worked well for us include:

- Always empathize rather than criticize. Do not pressure someone to declutter; this will just make them more resistant. Unfortunately, I learned the hard way!

- Ask your partner to help you with a small project, one where there will be no emotional attachment for them, such as a spice drawer. I bet you will have a laugh when you see some of those expiration dates! Make it a fun, quick, and simple task, and that way they will see just how easy it is to declutter.

- Create a "maybe" box. This is a really gentle approach, because the box acts as a temporary holding area for items that your partner is unsure about. Revisit the box after a set amount of time, and if your partner hasn't used the items, then it is time to let them go.

- Set boundaries. If your partner's clutter is impacting your daily life, then talk about it with them. Explain how it is affecting you, and come up with a solution that works for both of you.

Organizing

After the decluttering process, we get to the fun parts: organizing and folding.

Now that you have sorted your essential items into categories, you could simply put them back where they came from. Before doing so, have a look around and see if this makes sense. There may well be a better way to organize your items and create more effective spaces.

Game plan

Before putting items back where they were, take a step back and review the space. A really helpful approach, and what I refer to as the "game plan," is to list all the activities that take place within the space I am working on. It is important to do this because the key to organizing, and being able to maintain an organized space, is to store items close to where you use them. You are probably already doing this in some areas of your home. For example, where is your toothbrush? Chances are, it is near the bathroom sink. Storing items close to where you use them allows you to operate more efficiently: no more running downstairs to get items you use for cleaning the upstairs bathroom, or hunting for glasses that you only wear for reading in bed. It also means that finding and replacing items will become effortless. More often than not, we leave things out because it is too much effort to put them away.

As you progress in your organizing journey, you may start working on rooms in their entirety, one at a time, rather than smaller spaces. When you reach this point, I suggest you use the game plan before the decluttering process, so you have everything mapped out ready to go. This may be overwhelming at first, but you will learn as you go. The game plan is also the perfect tool to use if you are moving into a new home and want to plan where to put items as you unpack.

Here are two examples of how I organize rooms by activity

Bathroom

- Bathing (shampoo, conditioner, soap, towels, washcloths, loofah)

- Personal care (dental, shaving, hair styling, nail care, makeup)

- Cleaning (products, cloths, squeegee)

Bedroom

- Sleeping (spare blankets, duvets, pillows)

- Personal care (makeup, hair accessories, jewelery)

- TV/music (remote control, headphones)

- Reading (book, glasses, reading light)

The game plan is flexible because circumstances constantly change and evolve. For example, an activity might move from one room to another. You might decide to move gift wrapping materials from a drawer in the bedroom to a cabinet in the living room because that is where you wrap most of your gifts. Or, you may have to adapt to a larger lifestyle change. A week after Joey was born, I took a bad turn and ended up in the emergency room. While in the hospital, I asked Gavin to set up additional diaper changing areas in our living room and bedroom. Being on bed rest, with Gavin away for work, meant that I needed multiple stations around the home.

Storing items close to where they are used is a simple but very effective concept. Next, I am going to recommend a variety of storage solutions to help with this. I have included something to suit spaces and budgets of different sizes. My storage ideas are simple and versatile, and they can be used throughout your home. How and where you use them is not limited to the suggestions I have made.

Lazy Susans / turntables

Perfect for keeping an array of items in the foreground of a space. Suitable for kitchen, dining area, home office, bathroom, laundry, garage, coffee and tea station, arts and crafts, medicines, cleaning products.

Stackable drawers

Great for making use of both the height and depth of your space. Suitable for closet, bathroom, pantry, home office, garage, toys, arts and crafts, jewelery, medicines, pet supplies.

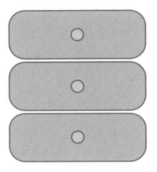

Collapsible baskets

Suitable for clothes, bedding, towels, blankets, laundry.

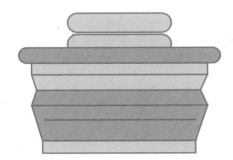

Drawer dividers / inserts

Perfect for containing items to a specific area in the drawer and for separating different items. Suitable for home office, kitchen, bathroom, bedroom, makeup, accessories, socks and underwear, arts and crafts, toys, tools, gift wrapping supplies.

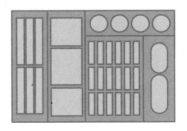

Stackable shoe storage

Perfect for keeping shoes contained and organized. Maximizes vertical space and keep shoes protected from dirt, dust, and moisture.

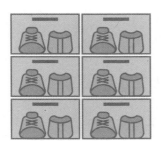

Door racks

Good for otherwise redundant spaces. Suitable for pantry, bathroom, closet, laundry, home office, playroom, garage, accessories, pet supplies, arts and crafts, cleaning products.

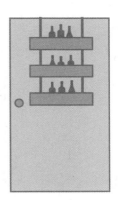

Storage baskets / bins with handles

Great for high shelves. Suitable for pantry, kitchen, living room, bathroom, laundry, playroom, home office, hallway, pet supplies, bed linen, arts and crafts.

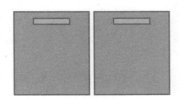

⊞ Top tip

When deciding which storage items to buy, make sure the containers are easy to clean and fit for purpose. Remember: "Buy well; buy once." And use either museum gel or drawer liners to stop your containers sliding around in your drawers or on your shelves.

Bedroom

I feel compelled to start our organizing journey in the bedroom. You, as my reader, are very important, and I want to start with a room that is just for you—perhaps a partner, too. When you close the bedroom door, you should be able to forget work, the family (I'm sorry, but we all need our own space), and any external forces playing on your mind. In the bedroom, you should find peace and solitude, joy and relaxation. And, ultimately, sleep. The bedroom is your space, nobody else's. It is time to own it.

Along with your boxes and bags labeled "throw away," "pass on," and "store" for the decluttering task, I suggest you bring a laundry basket with you into the bedroom (I hope it isn't in there already). The bedroom is often used as a dumping ground for things we are either too tired to put away or that have no specific home. Fill up your laundry basket and remove those random items from your bedroom.

Now, list all the activities that you perform in this space. You will need this later to help you decide where to store your items.

Flat surfaces

When you walk into the bedroom, your flat surfaces (dresser top, shelves, floor) are the first things you see, and they can significantly impact the entire ambience of the room. I suggest you organize them first.

You are aiming to keep your flat surfaces as clear as possible. The fewer items you have out, the less time you will spend cleaning. If something is essential for an activity you do in the bedroom, then it stays on the shelf or dresser. If it isn't, put it in one of your decluttering boxes.

Once you have cleared and organized your flat surfaces, your bedroom will not only be more visually appealing but it will also be a calmer environment in which you can relax and unwind.

Talking about flat surfaces, I was inspired by a DIY dusting spray I saw on TikTok. I have edited the ingredients to help you keep surfaces dust-free longer. When combined, these ingredients create a coating on the surface that repels dust. It really does work, but always patch test first.

- 1 cup water

- ½ cup vinegar

- 1 teaspoon olive oil

- 8 drops essential oil, to give your home a beautiful aroma (optional). If you have pets, please be aware that some essential oils are toxic for animals.

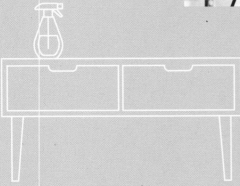

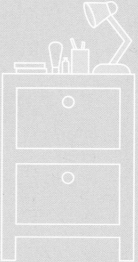

Night table

A night table provides great storage within the bedroom. However, what we store in this space should be organized thoughtfully to cultivate a peaceful environment. Bear this in mind when you are deciding what to keep in your night table.

What do you normally do prior to bed, or while lying either on or in it? Do you do your skincare routine, or moisturize your hands and feet? Do you wear glasses to read or watch TV? What items are essential for those activities?

My night table contains

- Current book
- Book light
- Glasses
- Cuticle set
- Cuticle oil
- Hand cream
- Pen and paper
- Pajamas

I have moved my phone charger from the night table into the living room. I was in the habit of scrolling on my phone before bed, and it wasn't good for me. I bought a three-in-one docking station to charge my phone, earbuds, and watch, and they all stay next to it when not charging or in use. It took a while to get into the habit of putting my phone in its new spot, but it is so worth it. It also means that my night table is less cluttered.

Storage suggestions

Fabric drawer inserts come in various sizes and are great for bedside drawers. They are perfect for organizing small items, such as accessories, cables, and glasses. Another cost-effective option is to repurpose small boxes.

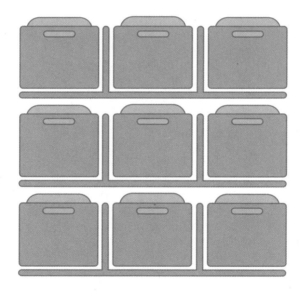

Q&A

"What type of night table do you recommend?"

I suggest a night table with at least one drawer. Nightstands without drawers may look great, but they encourage mess and clutter. You end up cramming all of your nighttime essentials on the top, which makes cleaning more time-consuming.

Under-bed storage

Some beds have no storage, and others have lots. Either way, do not use the space under your bed as a dumping ground. If your bed has drawers, this is the perfect place to store bed linen. It makes changing the bed a quicker and easier process. Extra blankets and cushions often fit nicely in these spaces, too.

Lift beds are great for storing seasonal clothes and footwear, as well as spare duvets and pillows. If you plan to store items for long periods, consider using vacuum storage bags. Dust and moths seem to be able to find their way into any space.

And let's not forget the space under a baby's crib. This is the perfect place to use a roll-out container to store spare crib linen and baby sleep sacks so they are easy to access if you need them during the night.

If there is no storage under your bed, try this blanket fold and store the blanket as a decorative piece on your bed or chair.

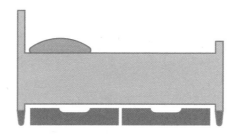

Blanket fold

1. Start with the blanket folded in half.

2. Fold from the left, and bring the fold two-thirds of the way over.

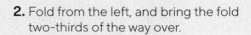
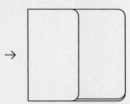

3. Fold from the right, over the top, and leave a small gap.

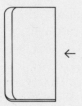

4. Fold from the top, to a little less than halfway down.

5. Fold up the bottom, and tuck in. Ready to put away or display.

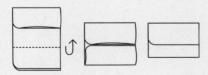

Clothing storage

To hang or to fold: that is the question. Many people choose which items to hang based on personal preference. There is nothing inherently wrong with this approach, but if you want to keep your clothes in better shape for longer, here are some things to consider.

Weight
To avoid stretching, distorting, or sagging, heavy fabrics should always be folded.

Material
Fabrics that are prone to creasing (silk, satin, cotton, linen) should be hung. Knitwear should be folded to stop it stretching. Items with embellishments (sequins, beading) should be folded in tissue paper for added protection.

Closet configuration/size
If you are short on hanging space, there are two options. You can either prioritize the items that you want to protect, or you can create a capsule wardrobe comprising your most commonly worn clothes.

This is how I organize my clothes, but you must prioritize what is important to you.

Hang

- Items that crease
- Shirts/blouses
- Jackets, blazers, and coats
- Dresses
- Lightweight sweaters
- Dress pants
- Skirts
- Pleated items

Fold

- T-shirts
- Heavy knitwear
- Casual pants and jeans
- Stretchy/slinky fabrics
- Heavily beaded/ embellished items

There are two effective ways to organize your clothes on a rod. You can hang like with like (tops, pants, dresses), or you can arrange your clothes by activity (work, casual, going-out). You could take this a step further and color code your items. Personally, I hang like with like, and my closet is organized from left to right in the order I select an outfit: coats, sweaters, tops, pants, dresses, and skirts. I do the same when organizing baby items and children's clothes, whether they are in a closet or drawer, or on a shelf.

On the following pages, you'll find a few of my viral hanging hacks to get you started.

Jeans

1. Lay jeans flat, zipper facing up, and fold in half, left leg over right. Place a hanger under the legs, a third of the way up.

2. Fold the bottom of the jeans down over the hanger.

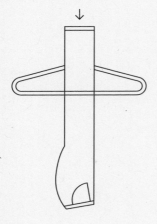

3. Bring the waistband up, and thread the hanger hook through a belt loop.

4. Hang the jeans so the labels are showing.

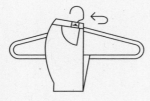

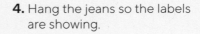
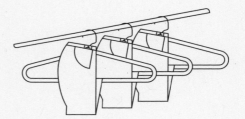

Long dresses

1. Lay the dress flat, with the back facing up. Place a hanger on top, a third of the way up.

2. Fold the bottom of the dress through the hanger. Depending on the style of the dress, you may need to fold in the sides of the dress first.

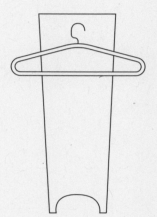

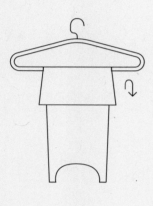

3. Bring the hanger down to the straps of the dress.

4. Place the straps on the hanger. Turn over the dress and hang.

Sweaters

1. Start with the sweater folded in half, and place a hanger on the diagonal.

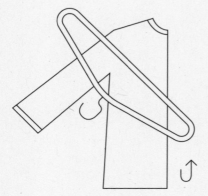

2. Fold up the bottom of the sweater through the hanger.

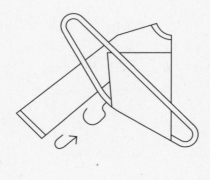

3. Fold the arms through the hanger.

4. Turn over the sweater and hang.

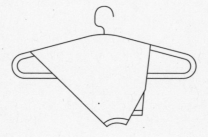

Creasing

When you fold something, you are bound to get some light creases. Most of these will drop out when you wear the garment. Here are some ways to keep creasing to a minimum:

- Avoid packing drawers and closets so full that it is hard to get things in and out. Give your items room to breathe.

- Do not make the folds too tight.

- If you use a dryer, take out your items as soon as the cycle finishes. Heat in the dryer helps remove creases from clothes, but if you leave them in there once the cycle has finished, any creases will set.

- Empty the laundry basket. Leaving clean laundry piled in the basket will cause creases.

- Leaving clothes flung over a chair, or in a pile at the bottom of your bed, will also cause creases. Put them away to avoid this.

- Never stack more than three items in a pile. As a pile increases in height, it also gets heavier. This will cause more pronounced creases to form in the items at the bottom of the pile.

Q&A

"How can I maximize my closet space?"

For double-rod hanging spaces, you could remove the bottom rod and insert a chest of drawers instead.

If you prefer to hang items, and your wardrobe has only one hanging rod, use a double hang closet rod. Simply hang it onto the existing rod, and this will immediately double your hanging space.

If the shelves in your closet are spaced far apart, move the top shelves up to reduce wasted air space. Use lightweight baskets with handles to contain items in this space. Remove low-level shelves, and insert a chest of drawers to maximize storage space below.

Use slimline, nonslip hangers, rather than bulky wooden or plastic ones. Matching hangers will create a more cohesive, uniform look that is less chaotic on the eye.

Add hanging shelves to the inside of your closet doors to create extra storage.

Use the inside of your closet door to create a "get ready" station. Hang items such as your everyday bag, jewelery, perfume, scarves, and belts, plus a mirror. With all your "essentials" in one place, it makes accessing and putting them away so much easier.

Alternate the direction of your shoes to gain some extra room.

Products that might help

- Collapsible linen baskets enable you to store items in a row, so you can see, access, and return them with ease. Also, collapsible baskets are easy to store when not in use.

- Shelf dividers are great for keeping piles of clothes tidy and separated.

- Clothes hanger connector hooks allow you to hang multiple items on one hanger.

⊠ *Top tip*

For clothes that have been worn but aren't ready for the laundry (the ones that get flung on a chair), place a self-adhesive towel rack on the inside of the closet door and hang your clothes there. Alternatively, attach a hook and hang a basket on the back of a door.

Drawers

I love a chest of drawers. I have removed the low-level shelves in our pantry and closets, and have replaced them all with chests of drawers. They are far more practical than deep shelves because you don't have to reach to the back to find something.

All the folds in the following section are designed so you can organize your items in a row in a drawer (or in a container on a shelf). When you remove one item, the others won't unravel. You can customize my folds to suit most spaces: either adjust where you make the fold, or fold in the sides a little more.

Remember: an effective space is one where you do not have to spend time refolding and resetting.

Additional storage suggestions

An ottoman or storage chest at the end of the bed can be used to store spare blankets and pillows.

As an alternative to a large shelving unit or cabinet, put up some floating shelves. These are less likely to compromise any natural light flowing through your bedroom.

There are numerous storage options for your wardrobe, including collapsible linen baskets, acrylic shelf dividers, bag hooks/dividers, self-adhesive hooks, hat hooks, door-hanging organizers, storage bag racks with pockets, stackable jewelery boxes, stackable shoe storage, and towel racks.

There are three organizing products that I use in drawers: expandable drawer dividers, fabric boxes (which come in many different sizes), and underwear organizers (which give each item their own spot).

"You can customize my folds to suit most spaces."

Let's fold

Jeans, joggers, leggings, and shorts

1. Lay the jeans flat, zipper facing up.

2. Lift the crotch, and fold it to the left. Fold the right leg over the left.

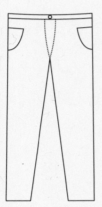

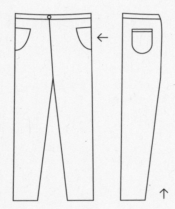

3. Fold up the bottom of the jeans, to just below the pocket.

4. Fold the top down, then fold the bottom up, and tuck it into the opening.

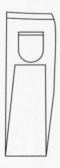

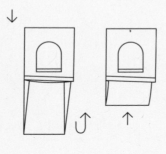

5. Store your folded jeans, with the labels visible, in a drawer or in a container on a shelf.

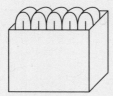

✳ *Top tip*

If you find the tuck part is too tight, simply pull the sides of the garment away from the center to create more room.

Underwear

1. Lay the underwear flat.

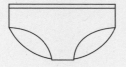

2. Fold in the left side, and the right side over it.

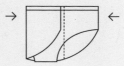

3. Fold the top down, and tuck in the bottom. Ready to put away.

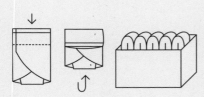

✳ *Top tip*

Bras with padding should be lined up to stop them losing their shape.

Long socks

1. Place one sock on top of the other.

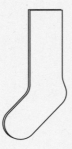

2. Fold in the heels.

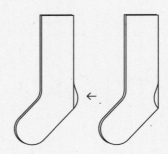

3. Fold up the toe of one sock. Fold down the tops of both socks over it.

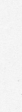

4. Fold up the remaining sock toe, and tuck it in. Ready to put away.

No-show socks

1. Lay the socks flat, and place one inside the other.

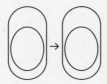

2. Fold up the bottom, and tuck it into the top. Ready to put away.

Ankle socks

1. Lay the socks flat with the sole facing up. Place one on top of the other.

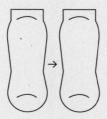

2. Fold up the toe of one sock. Fold down the tops of both socks over it.

3. Fold up the remaining sock toe, and tuck it in.

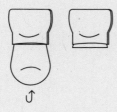

Sweaters, hoodies, and shirts

For a hoodie, fold the hood down first, and then follow the steps for folding a sweater.

1. Lay the sweater flat. Fold in both sleeves, so each cuff is in line with the opposite side of the collar.

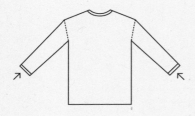

2. Fold each side into the middle.

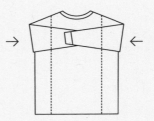

3. Fold down the top.

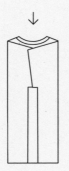

4. Fold up the bottom, and tuck in. Ready to put away.

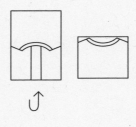

Jerseys and golf shirts

1. Lay the item flat, and fold in both sides.

2. Fold up the bottom of the shirt halfway, and then roll. I prefer to roll this type of clothing because it tends to be slippery.

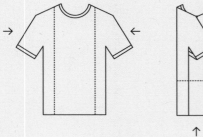

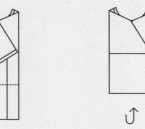

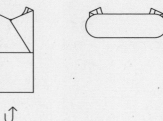

Top tip

This fold is great for any material that tends to have a mind of its own, and it can also be used on other items. Many people use this method to store shirts in a drawer. How you chose to implement the folds within your home is your choice. Try them out and see what works best.

Sports bras without padding

1. Lay the item flat, with the front facing down.

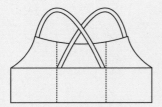

2. Fold in each side.

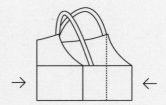

3. Fold up from the bottom.

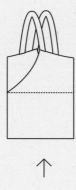

4. Tuck in the straps. Ready to put away.

Top tip

Sports bras with padding should be hung or stored like normal bras.

T-shirts

1. Lay the T-shirt flat, with the front facing down. Fold in one side.

2. Fold in the other side.

3. Fold down the top of the T-shirt halfway.

4. Fold the bottom up and over it.

5. Turn the T-shirt around, so the opening is closer to you. Tuck the end fold in. Ready to put away.

Pajamas: winter option

1. Fold the pants in half, and lay the pajama top flat.

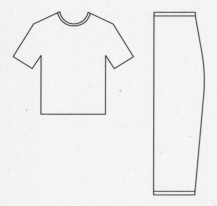

2. Place the T-shirt face up. Hold just below the armpit on each side and lift up.

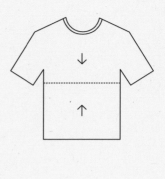

3. Place it down, folded, with the neckline underneath.

4. Fold in the left side, followed by the right.

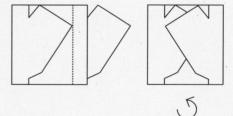

5. Fold the top over once more, so the pajama top fits on the pajama pants.

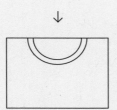

6. Place the pajama top on the pants.

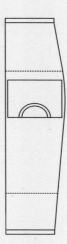

7. Fold the top of the pants down over the pajama top.

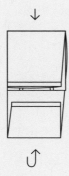

8. Fold up the legs, and then tuck the bottom edge into the opening. Ready to put away.

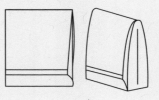

Pajamas: summer option

1. Lay the T-shirt flat, with the front facing down, and lay the shorts on top.

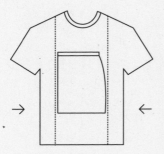

2. Fold in both sides of the T-shirt over the shorts.

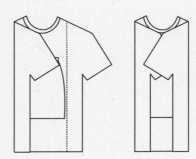

3. Fold down the top, and fold up the bottom.

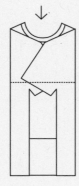

4. Tuck in the bottom, behind the neck of the T-shirt. Ready to put away.

Shelves

Shelving space can be used effectively so you can easily see, access, and return all of your items without having to manage and reset unruly piles. Over the next few pages are a few alternative folds for storing your items on shelves.

Jeans and joggers

1. Lay jeans flat, with the zipper facing up.

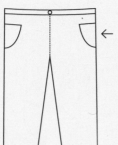

2. Fold the right leg over the left.

3. Fold up the bottom, a third of the way.

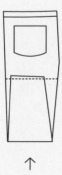

4. Fold the top down and over it. Ready to put away.

Hoodie roll

1. Lay the hoodie flat, with the front facing up.

2. Fold the arms across the front.

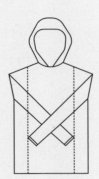

3. Fold in the sides.

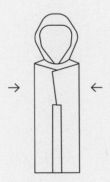

4. Roll the hoodie from the bottom up, and tuck the roll into the hood. Ready to put away.

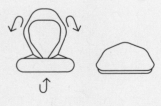

Baby and children's clothes

Joggers and shorts

I use the same technique for both joggers and shorts.

1. Fold the right leg over the left.

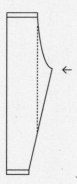

2. Fold in the crotch.

3. Fold down the top halfway.

4. Fold up the bottom, and tuck it into the opening. Ready to put away.

Tights

1. Lay the tights flat, and fold the right leg over the left.

2. Fold up the legs, so they are in line with the crotch.

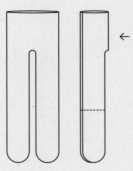

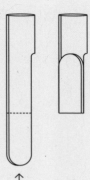

3. Fold the top down and over this. Fold up the bottom, and tuck it into the waistband. Ready to put away.

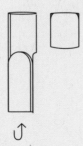

Onesies and sleepers

1. Lay the onesie flat. Fold up the bottom section.

2. Fold in the arms, and bring the top down over the bottom.

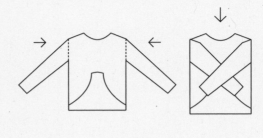

3. Fold over the right side, and tuck the left side into it. Ready to put away.

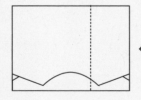

Onesies and sleepers (flat fold)

1. Lay the item flat, with the front facing down. Fold in the arms.

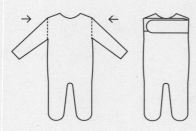

2. Fold up the legs.

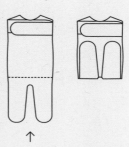

3. Fold the top down over the legs. Ready to put away.

Sleep sacks

1. Lay the sleep sack flat.

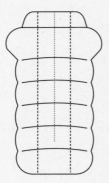

2. Fold over the left side.

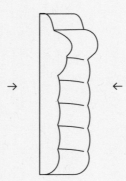

3. Fold over the right side, making sure it overlaps. Fold up the bottom a third of the way.

4. Fold down the top and tuck in.

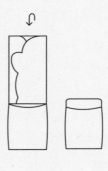

Top tip

If you have young children who attend daycare, you have most likely experienced mornings when they want to change their outfit multiple times, or refuse to put anything on. Try preparing their outfits in advance. On top of the dresser in our boys' room, I have three containers: one for each of the days they attend daycare. My boys choose three outfits at the start of the week, and we put them in the containers. This allows them to select their outfit, but only from one of the three options.

Diaper bag

Diaper bags come in all shapes and sizes. Whichever style you choose, it is essential to organize your bag.

- If your bag doesn't have compartments, buy an insert or use small cosmetic bags or mesh zipper bags to organize your items. Label each bag by activity: diaper changing, clothes, toys, feeding, and so on. You want to keep items separate, so they are easy to find when you need them.

- Replenish diapers, wipes, outfits, snacks, and so on as soon as you get home. Do it before you are distracted by other tasks and forget.

- Hand sanitizer and a small first aid kit are a must.

- If your child uses a pacifier, keep a spare one in an outside pocket, so it is quick to grab when you need it. Store it in a case.

- Pack a change of clothes (see page 97 if you think it won't fit in the bag), snacks, and fluids for yourself. You are important, too.

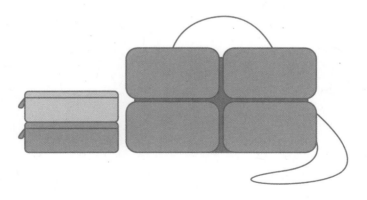

Outfit fold (babies and toddlers)

1. Using the same folds as for winter pajamas (see page 84), place the folded top on the folded pants.

2. Fold down the top. Fold up the bottom, and tuck it into the opening.

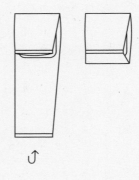

The outfit is neatly folded together, so you can always locate a change of clothes.

Top tip

You can use this fold to plan outfits for a vacation. That way, each day you have outfits prepared and ready to use. We also use this method when taking spare clothes to the pool or beach. I find laying items out together helps me remember everything.

Outfit fold (adults)

1. Lay the shirt flat, with the front facing down. Fold the bottom of the garment underneath, approximately 3 in (8 cm).

2. Fold the leggings in half and place them on top.

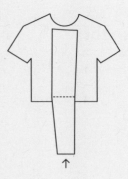

3. Fold in both sides of the shirt, and make sure they overlap.

4. You can either fold or roll, from the top to the bottom.

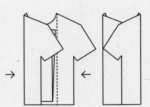

5. As you are folding or rolling, you will see the fold you created at the start. Place your hands inside this, and take it around the item until it secures the fold.

Bed linen

I store my bed linen in a drawer under our bed. I use the folding methods described below, but I lay the linen flat so it fits in the drawer. If you use a linen closet, airing cupboard, or shelving space, store items vertically, in a horizontal row, so they are easy to see, access, and put back.

Fitted sheets

1. Lay the fitted sheet on a flat surface with the hole facing up.

2. Take the bottom two corners and tuck them inside the elasticized hole.

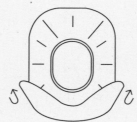

3. Fold them up to the top, and place them inside the top two corners.

4. Fold in the sides, starting with the left. Fold the right over the left.

5. Fold up from the bottom.

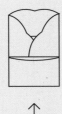

6. Turn the sheet around, and tuck in the end. Ready to put away.

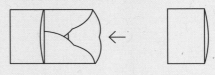

7. If you want to achieve a smaller end product, make the folds smaller. Fold from the left, then from the right, and then bring the right over again so that it overlaps.

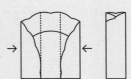

Bedding bundles

1. Fold your duvet cover in half, and then in half again.

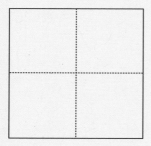

2. After following steps 1, 2, and 3 of the fitted sheet fold, place the sheet on top of the duvet cover.

3. Fold in the left side, and then bring the right side over it.

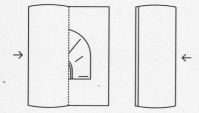

4. Fold from the bottom up or top down, and tuck in the other end. Fold your pillowcases, and place them in the pocket. Ready to put away.

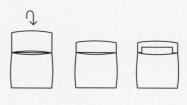

Reverse pillowcase fold

1. Turn one pillowcase inside out, and place it so the envelope closure is at the bottom.

2. Place one set of folded bed linen inside the pillowcase.

3. Fold the pillowcase up and over the bundle, so it exposes the envelope closure.

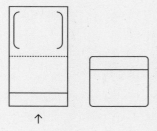

4. Use the envelope closure to secure the bundle. Ready to put away.

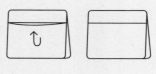

Children's bed linen

Depending on the age of your children, you may not want to store their bed linen in bundles. You may prefer to keep the fitted sheets, duvet covers, and sheet protectors separate, so they are readily available in case of accidents. I use the fitted sheet fold for both the sheet and the protector, and store them separately in clearly labeled baskets. For pillowcases and duvet covers, you can use either the bundle fold or the reverse pillowcase fold.

Duvet covers

1. Lay the duvet cover flat, and fold the bottom under about 24 in (60 cm).

2. Fold in from the left, and bring the right side over the top.

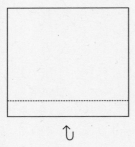

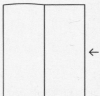

Top tip

If you have a spare duvet and pillowcase set that is used together, place the pillows flat in the center of the duvet after step 1 and complete the fold, keeping your spares in one place.

3. Fold down from the top, twice.

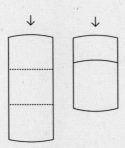

4. Flip over the duvet cover, and it will expose the first fold you created.

5. Place your arms inside the pocket, and take it over the opposite corner. Ready to put away.

Storage suggestions

Use collapsible baskets to store your bed linen in a row, either in sets or by type. If you have plenty of space, I recommend organizing your linen by bed size: all king-size sheets, fitted sheets, and duvet covers on one shelf, all doubles on the shelf below, and so on.

Alternatively, acrylic shelf dividers will allow you to see items on the shelf more easily, and will create distinct sections. Items of bed linen often look the same, so clear labeling is essential.

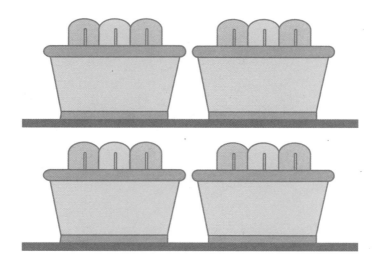

Q&A

"How many sets of bed linen do you recommend?"

Two sets for adult beds. One on the bed, and the other in the wash. You may wish to have three sets, but you don't need any more than that.

For younger children, I recommend three sets. Accidents and illnesses happen, and you don't want to be caught off guard.

"Use collapsible baskets to store your bed linen."

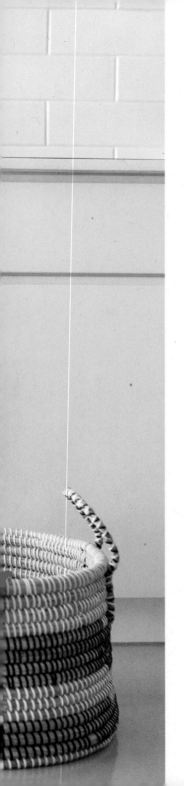

Laundry

Although I share a lot of folding techniques on social media, I do not like doing the laundry any more than the next person. Therefore, I try to make my laundry routine as efficient as possible.

A laundry space tends to fall into one of two categories. It is either highly organized and functional, or it is a mishmash of dirty and clean laundry, with odd socks poking out from underneath the washing machine. Whether you have a small or large space, organizing it so it works well for you will make doing the laundry more enjoyable.

If you are lucky enough to have a separate laundry or utility room, what activities do you do there? Washing, drying, and folding, I presume—but is there anything else? Break down the room by activity. This will give you a clear picture of how you need the space to function.

You do, of course, need to store all your laundry detergents, softeners, dryer balls, and so on within easy reach of your machine(s). Because so many laundry products have busy labels and colorful packaging, I suggest you decant your most frequently used products so the space feels less chaotic. If decanting isn't your thing, then group items in broad categories (washing, drying, cleaning products), and store them in containers that are easy to clean (a spillage is inevitable at some point). Label the containers clearly.

Having a folding station close to the dryer is ideal, but in many homes this isn't possible. I fold as I go, and put items straight into the drawers or closet.

Odd socks should be put in a designated area. This could be a basket or a small hanging line. I peg odd socks on a line, so I can make a pair as soon as the other one turns up. I have attached two self-adhesive hooks under a shelf and tied a little rope to them to create a mini clothesline. Three months is the maximum time on the line! After that, you could repurpose the sock as an ice pack cover, or use it as a glove to clean out tricky nooks and crannies.

A final thought. To prevent mold and mildew growing in the washing machine, always leave the door open. This allows moisture to evaporate and air to circulate inside the machine. And don't forget to clean your machine regularly.

Q&A

"How do you keep your towels soft?"

Cut back on the detergent, and wash on a high temperature. Swap out the softener for white vinegar. Wash towels separately from other items, and don't overload the dryer. If the dryer is too full, your towels will come out stiff and matted.

Q&A

"How do you stay on top of laundry?"

I include doing the laundry as part of my everyday routine.

Morning

My first "chore" of the day is making the bed. Next, I put a load of washing in the machine, and go for a run.

During the day

Dry, fold, and put the washing away. I mostly work from home, so I am able to do this during the day. If you work away from home, set a timer on the washing machine so the cycle finishes at a time when you will be able to dry the clothes. I tidy and clean as needed. This way, mess doesn't accumulate. If something is dirty, I clean it. If something is messy, I tidy it. I prefer to do little and often, but that is just my way of working.

Evening

Our nightly routine sets us up for the next day. Everyone in the house gets involved.

Before dinner, we put away all the toys, and have a little downtime. Right after dinner, we clean up, do the dishes, wipe down surfaces, clean the stove and sink, and start the dishwasher. We have some family time, before it's bath, story, and bed for the boys. I do my face—cleanse, tone, and moisturize—in the bathroom while the kids are in the bath. Once the boys are in bed, either Gavin or I will vacuum and mop. Then it's time to relax and unwind. Later, one of us will unload the dishwasher once the cycle is finished.

Storage suggestions

Use glass containers for laundry pods and dryer balls, and refillable clear pump bottles for liquids. Store the bottles on a turntable for ease of access.

Collapsible laundry baskets take up less space in the laundry room, and narrow carts on wheels are handy because they slot into small spaces.

A wall-mounted drying rack is the perfect place to hang delicate items. Many of these racks can be folded up when not in use.

Attach magnetic trash cans and racks to the side of the washing machine or dryer. They can be used to collect lint and other laundry debris, and to store miscellaneous items, such as a dustpan and brush, or even those odd socks.

Install a wall-mounted ironing organizer to keep the iron and ironing board off the floor and out of view.

Use a tool organizer, mounted to a wall or door, to keep brooms and mops off the floor, and to stop them falling over.

⊞ *Top tip*

A load a day keeps those piles at bay. If you have a large household, working a load of laundry into your daily routine will help you keep on top of it.

Bathroom

The bathroom is one of the most frequently used spaces in the home, so you must make it as functional as possible. The last thing you want is to feel overwhelmed or stressed when getting ready to start your day or winding down for bed.

As the bathroom is typically smaller than other spaces in the home, it may not be possible to store all items where everyone uses them. An effective alternative is to allocate designated areas for each person to store their belongings. Depending on their age, they can organize their own space based on their individual needs. You can still keep frequently used items—towels, shampoo, toothpaste—close to where they are used.

Flat surfaces

As in the bedroom, keep flat surfaces as free from clutter as possible. Whether you share a bathroom or have the space to yourself (lucky you), it will always be a place that requires frequent cleaning. The clearer your flat surfaces, the quicker they are to clean. I'm not suggesting you move your toothbrush away from the sink: it should be kept close to where you use it. But, empty bottles, used face cloths, loose hair accessories—these items have no place on your flat surfaces. If you like to keep skincare products on the countertop, put them in a small storage basket.

We don't want to be so clinical that the bathroom feels sterile and uninviting. Adding a small decorative tray with a few personal touches, and maybe a washcloth roll or two, can add to the overall aesthetic of the space. It is practical, too. A tray keeps items contained, and when it's time to clean, you only have to lift up one item rather than several.

Washcloth roll

1. Lay the washcloth flat on the diagonal.

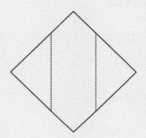

2. Fold each side into the middle so they overlap.

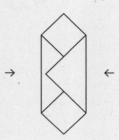

3. Lift up the washcloth from the center, and it will fold naturally. Place it down.

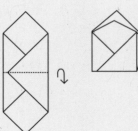

4. Roll from the bottom to the top, and tuck in the end. Ready to put away.

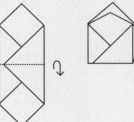

Drawers

Select organizers that fit the size and shape of the drawers in your bathroom. Store your most commonly used items in the drawers closest to the top, and also toward the front of the drawer itself.

Use small boxes or baskets, or recycle containers or jars, to store small loose items, such as hair accessories, toothpicks, and razor heads. Personally, I like to reuse candle jars. An easy and effective way to recycle these is to pour hot water into the container. The wax will melt and rise to the surface. Wait for it to cool, and then lift it out and throw it in the trash. Do not pour the melted wax down the drain; we don't want to cause a blockage. Remove any residue, and away you go.

Cabinets

Bathroom cabinets often have cluttered shelves, which make it hard to find what you want in a hurry. Whether your cabinet is large or small, the key to organizing is to make effective use of the space you are working with. One simple way to do this is to reposition the shelves, particularly if you have tall toiletries to accommodate. Label any containers clearly, so all family members know where to find and replace items. And always store the items you use most often at the front.

Storage suggestions

In low-level cabinets, use stackable drawers for your smaller items. They make the most of both the depth and height of the cabinet space. Things do not get lost at the back of the cabinet, and wasted air space is reduced. Items are easy to access and put back, which makes maintaining your space easier. For larger items, use baskets and bins in your low-level cabinets, and choose ones that are easy to clean. If space allows, insert a shelf riser to create an additional layer.

For high-level cabinets, use storage that is lightweight and has a handle, so it is easy to pull out and put back. Avoid using stackable drawers in spaces above eye level, because you won't be able to see what is in the top drawer without removing the drawer itself.

If you have large cabinets in the bathroom, a two-tiered pull-out shelf unit is a simple but effective storage solution. If you need to work around plumbing, you could use a tiered corner shelf.

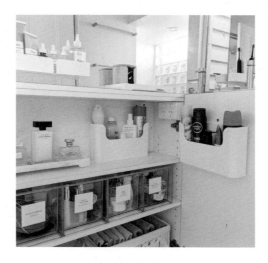

Under-sink units

Save yourself some time and store bathroom cleaning products where you need them: in the bathroom. If you have a cabinet under the sink, this is the perfect place to put them. Use a turntable for liquids and sprays, and a container for cloths and brushes.

Bath toys

A simple way to keep bath toys organized is to hang a suction mesh net on the inside of the bathtub or shower. This allows the toys to air dry, while excess water runs directly down the drain.

Shower enclosures

The most effective way to organize your shower is to use a shower caddy. There are many different types available: hanging caddies, corner caddies, caddy baskets, adjustable caddies, and even spring-loaded tension rod caddies. They all serve the same purpose, so it really comes down to individual preference.

Personally, I avoid open-shelf storage in the shower. It looks good, but shower caddies are usually multifunctional, with hooks for loofahs and sponges, and a place to store your razor. Caddy baskets will contain your items and stop them toppling onto the floor. Whatever you decide, make sure the item is rust proof, durable, and sturdy.

I also keep a squeegee in the shower to quickly wipe excess water and soap residue from the shower walls.

Medicine and first aid

It is important to avoid storing medicines in areas where the temperature fluctuates, or where there is high humidity. Some medicines might not react well to these conditions. A cool, dry, dark area is the ideal spot.

I store our medicines in the kitchen, away from heat sources, because we all spend a lot of time there. Choose a space that makes sense to you and that is out of reach of children and pets.

Storage suggestions

- Select containers that are light and easy to put in and pull out of spaces.

- Label your containers in broad categories, such as sun, cold and flu, pain relief, kids.

- Have a separate container for items that are used frequently and that you may need to access quickly. This would include bandages, ibuprofen, inhaler, thermometer, and antiseptic cream.

- If you take several medications each day, a pill organizer will help you keep track of what you need to take and when.

Folds for the bathroom

It will come as no surprise that I love folding towels. Whether it is for guests or for yourself, I truly believe that adding small, simple touches can really elevate your space. After all, why shouldn't we enjoy a touch of luxury in our homes?

Towel tuck

When it comes to folding towels, there is no one-size-fits-all approach. What works best for you will depend on the size of your bathroom, your storage options, and your personal preferences. Experiment with these different techniques to find the one that is the best fit.

The tuck fold is my favorite, and it is a very simple and effective way to fold towels. The beauty of this fold is that it can be customized so your towel fits in any size space and it won't unravel, even if you are rummaging around. With this method, you can store towels in a row (always a winner in my eyes), so your towel closet, shelf, or drawer is easier to maintain.

1. Fold your towel in half.

2. Take the seamed edges (right), and fold them back toward the center.

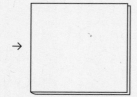

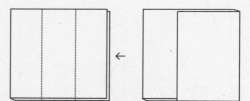

3. Fold the left side up and over.

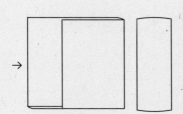

4. Fold down the top. This fold will determine the size of the end product. Make this fold smaller if you need to.

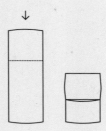

5. Either fold or roll up the towel, and tuck the bottom edge into the opening. Ready to put away.

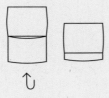

⊞ *Top tip*

This fold is also useful for transporting towels in a bag, for example if you head to the gym or go backpacking, because it prevents them from coming undone. Roll the towels into the tuck to create a more compact end product that will fit in a bag.

Guest towels (hanging fold)

1. Lay the towel flat, and fold up
the bottom about 3 in (8 cm).

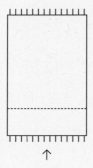

2. Then fold it back under
by the same amount.

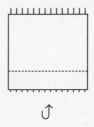

3. Fold in the left side, and then
the right side, so they overlap.

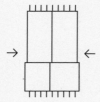

4. Lift the left side, and tuck the right side
underneath.

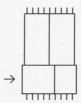

5. Turn it over, and place on a towel rack.
Add a decorative touch.

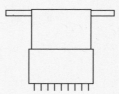

Guest towels (flat fold)

1. Lay the towel flat, and fold under the bottom about 3 in (8 cm).

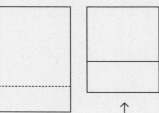

2. Fold in the left side, and then the right side, so they overlap.

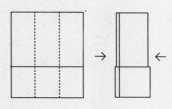

3. Fold up from the bottom to just over halfway.

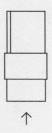

4. Turn the towel around, and tuck in the final part.

5. Add some decorative pieces for guests.

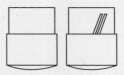

Washcloths

1. Lay the washcloth flat, and fold in the left side.

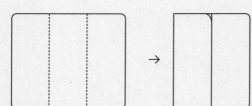

2. Fold the right side over the left. Fold the top down, and the bottom up.

3. Tuck the bottom into the opening.

4. Add a decorative touch for guests.

Viral towel roll

1. Start with the towel folded in half.

2. Fold in the bottom right corner.

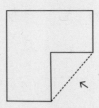

3. Fold the top left corner over this.

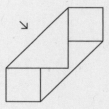

4. Lift the towel from the center, and then place it back down, folded.

5. Roll from the bottom to the top.

6. Tuck in the point.

We have already covered all of the storage options, so I have a top tip here instead. A motion sensor trash can is a good idea in the bathroom. The hands-free operation is not only convenient, but it also eliminates the need to touch the trash can and, therefore, reduces the spread of germs.

Q&A

"I have a really small bathroom; how can I use the space better?"

Have a look at any unused space, and think about how you could use it to best suit your needs.

Making the most of vertical space can really help with storage issues. A towel rack or suction hook on the back of a door is a good way to keep towels off the floor, and both are quick and easy to install. Suction hooks can also be used on shower walls or doors.

You could mount a hanging shower caddy to hold all sorts of items on a wall, inside a cabinet, or behind a door. Although caddies are marketed for shower use, they can be hung elsewhere.

Consider using the space above the toilet.

You could install some shelves or a cabinet there. Or perhaps you could use a ladder-style shelf unit that leans against the wall. Any of these storage solutions will provide extra space for toilet paper, towels, and other bathroom essentials.

Install magnetic strips for smaller items such as tweezers, nail clippers, and scissors, making them easy to access and put back.

Rolling carts are very versatile. If you love makeup and hair products but share the bathroom with others, you may not be able to keep all of your items in the bathroom permanently. A rolling cart can be easily moved from one place to the next.

Kitchen

When organizing and maintaining an effective space, the kitchen often presents the greatest challenge. It is a high traffic area, and it commonly serves as a multipurpose space. We also bring a lot of new items into the kitchen each week. For these reasons, I am going to take a different approach here, and break the space down into activities.

Game plan

Common activities in the kitchen include preparing food, cooking, putting away dishes, storing food items, and washing dishes and cleaning. You might also use this space for other things, such as homework, crafting, working from home, and DIY projects.

For now, let's focus on the common activities, because organizing these will help you optimize the effectiveness of your kitchen space. As part of the game plan, I'll also recommend storage solutions after each activity. No matter the layout of your kitchen, there are options to suit all spaces and budgets.

It is important to consider how you would like your family members to use the kitchen space. Placement is key. For example, if you have young children and want them to be able to get snacks, plates and bowls, water bottles, and so on, you will need to store these items lower down, where they can access them with ease. And if you want to keep certain items out of reach, place them in the upper cabinets or on higher shelves.

Preparing food

To create an efficient food preparation area, you want a dedicated place where you can wash, prepare, mix, and season food. A surface area that is close to the sink, refrigerator, and food storage cabinets is ideal. This may not be possible, so prioritize whatever makes most sense based on your own cooking habits. If you use fresh produce frequently, then your food preparation area should be next to the sink; if you bake a lot, next to the storage cabinets might be better. Wherever you choose, store all your food preparation utensils and equipment in cabinets and drawers close to this space. Keep surfaces clear so you have enough room to prepare your food.

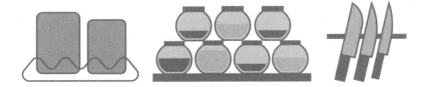

Storage suggestions

- Store cutting boards in a magazine file holder (from an office supply store). Attach it to the inside of a cabinet using double-sided tape, or place it on a shelf.

- Organize your spices in a way that makes sense to you. This could be alphabetically, according to how often you use them, or something else.

- To save space on countertops, get rid of your bulky knife block. Instead, attach a magnetic strip to the wall, and store your knives there.

- Use a pegboard organizer or a pot lid rack inside a drawer to keep food containers under control. Decide whether you want to store them with the lids on or off. I prefer lids on, so each container has its corresponding lid readily available.

- Nest your mixing bowls together, and use a self-adhesive hook to hang measuring spoons so they never go astray.

Cooking

Store pots, pans, baking sheets, oven dishes, and cooking utensils close to the stove and oven. Depending on the size and layout of your kitchen, you might also want to store cooking oils and commonly used spices close by. If you are similar to me and have no storage space near the stove and oven, choose a dedicated area within your kitchen and store all of these items together. That way, when you are cooking, you will only need to visit one space to get all your items.

 Top tip

Planning meals on a weekly basis will save money and reduce food waste. I use a magnetic fridge planner that has a section for meals and a shopping list. Planning meals at the start of the week removes some of the pressure throughout the rest of the week.

Storage suggestions

- It is natural for us to stack pots, pans, and baking sheets on top of each other to save space. But this makes it awkward to get the items in and out, and may also scratch and damage nonstick surfaces. A simple, cost-effective way to double your shelf space is to add a shelf riser to your cabinet. You can then sit each pan separately, and access them all easily with one hand.

- If you have enough room, use a pot and pan organizer to keep your pieces separate. There are shelf or rack options to suit a variety of spaces. Such organizers make pans easy to see, access, and put back.

- If you store pots and pans in a drawer, use a pegboard drawer organizer to stop them moving around when you open and close the drawer. Alternatively, you could use an expandable pan holder or rack to keep your items in place.

- Store your baking sheets upright, like books on a shelf, so they are easy to access and put back. An expandable holder will help you organize them by size or function.

- Use a small decorative tray or turntable for oils, depending on how many you have.

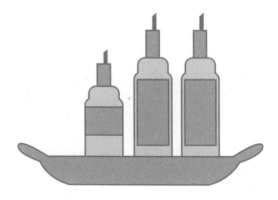

Putting away tableware

Everyday dishes

I recommend that you choose one of the following two options. Store your everyday plates, bowls, mugs, and glasses close to the dishwasher and/or sink, to simplify the process of putting them away. Alternatively, store these items close to where you use them: for example, mugs close to the coffee machine, and plates close to where you serve food. Typically, I tend to handle more items when unloading the dishwasher than I do when serving food, so I prefer the first option.

Storage suggestions

- As mentioned, use a shelf riser to double the space in your cabinets. If possible, avoid nesting different-sized bowls and plates together.

- Try not to stack too many plates or bowls one on top of the other. It makes them difficult to access, and they are more likely to break.

- Use a plate holder to store plates in a row, so each one is easy to access.

- Add a pegboard organizer to your drawers to separate plates and bowls.

Formal dinnerware

Unless you use formal dinnerware every night, store serving dishes and utensils, napkins, place mats, and tablecloths close to where you entertain guests. This might be in the kitchen—but ensure they are not occupying prime real estate—or it might be in a separate dining area.

If your formal dinnerware is not used on a daily basis, prioritize the storage space in your kitchen for the essential items that you use regularly. We keep our place mats laid out on the dining table, because they are used at every meal. It also stops family members placing random items on the dining table and creating a clutter hot spot.

Storage suggestions

- If you have open shelving or you wish to display your dinnerware, plate racks and stands offer an elegant and space-saving storage solution.

- Use drawer dividers and small containers to store smaller items, such as napkins, napkin rings, and serving utensils. They will help keep these pieces organized.

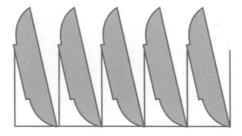

Storing food

Let's split this activity into three categories: cold goods (refrigerator), cold goods (freezer), and dry goods.

Cold goods (refrigerator)

Remember: you don't need complex systems. The idea is to create effective spaces that are easy to maintain.

Think of the main foods you store in the refrigerator, and allocate one container to each category. You don't want the refrigerator to look and feel cluttered, so I suggest using a uniform set of containers. Label them clearly.

I use broad categories for items in my refrigerator. They work so well for me that I haven't changed the way I organize my refrigerator since 2018.

- Yogurts
- Eggs
- Condiments
- Cheese
- Deli

- Leftovers
- Treats
- Meat
- Fish

All vegetables and fruits are stored in the lower crisper drawer, and I always have some space left over for other items.

Storage suggestion

- Use a turntable for condiments in the refrigerator. It will help you access all items easily and stop you forgetting about the ones at the back.

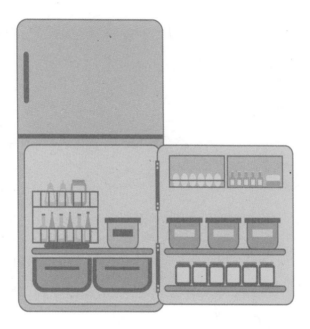

⊠ *Top tip*

Put a small bowl of baking soda on a shelf in the refrigerator to remove odors naturally. Change it every two or three months, depending on how often you clean out your refrigerator.

Cold goods (freezer)

Similar to the refrigerator, keep the categories for your
frozen goods broad: vegetables, meat, desserts, for
example. If your freezer has different compartments or
sections, assign a different category of food to each one.

   You don't need to decant packaged food into different
containers. To save space, simply fold boxes and cut and
tie bags as shown on the opposite page.

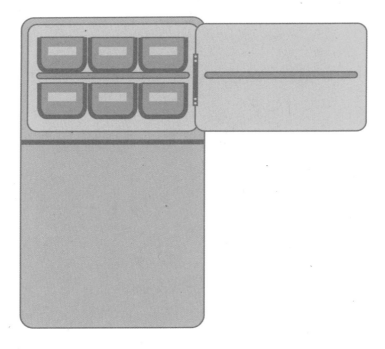

Bags

1. Cut down the center of the bag.

2. Lift up the bag, and tie the sides together.

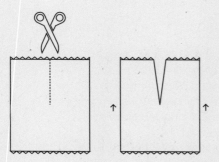

Boxes

1. Start with the box completely open, and then fold three flaps down and into the box, keeping one of the longer edged unfolded.

2. Pinch in the box on both sides, and fold in the remaining flap.

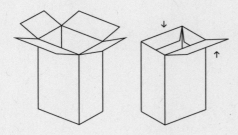

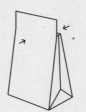

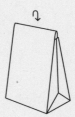

Dry goods

Whether you store dry goods in a cabinet or pantry, you need to create categories that make sense to you. For example, you could categorize by food stuff—grains and cereals, snacks and treats, pasta and rice—or by meal type: breakfast, lunch, dinner. Or, it could be a combination of both.

Irrespective of how you categorize dry goods, use your lower shelves for heavy and bulky items, store more frequently used items at eye level, and place lighter items on higher shelves. Reserve the topmost shelves for the items you use the least.

"Create categories that make sense to you"

Storage suggestions

- When organizing deep cabinets, select appropriate storage options to make best use of the space. You want to use both the depth and the height, so I suggest deep baskets or containers to use the depth, and under-shelf storage baskets to use the height.

- Use open baskets or clear containers for packets and snacks. I like to use clear storage so I can see, at a glance, what needs replacing when writing my shopping list.

- Stackable bamboo containers are great, but don't stack two of the same size one on top of the other. Put a large container on the bottom, and a smaller one on top, so contents in the bottom container are easier to access.

- Store canned goods on tiered shelving, so each can is visible and easy to access.

- Add a turntable for bottled items.

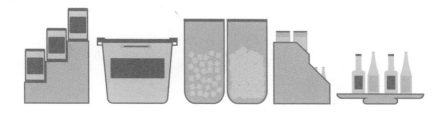

Decanting

At this stage, we need to talk about decanting. It can be beneficial and practical in certain situations, but you don't want to go overboard and create more work for yourself. Ultimately, it comes down to personal preference. To help you make an informed decision, I have compiled a list of the pros and cons of decanting.

Pros

- Bulky packaging can be removed to free up valuable space.

- Differently shaped and sized packaging can be discarded to eliminate clutter.

- Decanting can help maintain the freshness of some items, protecting them from air, moisture, and light, which can impact their quality and flavor.

- By transferring snacks into containers, you can control portion sizes.

- Tags or labels can be added, so items can be identified easily, and everyone knows where they belong. Labels also help children recognize letters and words.

- If you use clear containers, you will be able to see stock levels at all times.

- Transferring liquids into containers that have dispensers or spouts can make them less messy to use.

- Most containers are more visually appealing than packaging.

Cons

- If you are not recycling your own jars, the initial costs of purchasing containers can be high.

- Containers may not be airtight, and food may become stale faster.

- It is time-consuming to decant items, wash containers, check stock levels, and refill them.

- You have to create additional storage space for back stock. You also have to continue to monitor back stock against decanted stock.

- Space constraints may mean you need to stack or store containers one behind another. This may:
  - Make it difficult to access items at the back or bottom of a cupboard, and you may need to move multiple containers to access the one you want
  - Mean that some containers are less visible, and some items may get forgotten or overlooked
  - Create unsteadiness if containers aren't nested properly, or if the containers aren't designed for stacking
  - Apply pressure to lids and seals, potentially compromising their effectiveness

Storage suggestions

- Jam jars or pasta sauce jars can be washed and repurposed as storage containers. In the kitchen, you could use them to decant your spices, or any dry goods that you use in smaller quantities.

- Add a turntable to your cupboard for containers you access frequently.

Washing dishes and cleaning

I recommend keeping the area around the sink free from clutter. Limit the items stored next to the sink to dishwashing essentials, and replace large dish and hand soap bottles with smaller, reusable pump containers. Use a decorative tray to store these containers, or buy a sink caddy organizer, which also keeps scourers and cloths contained. When cleaning, it is much easier to lift one tray, rather than multiple bottles placed haphazardly around the sink area.

The cabinet under the kitchen sink is one of my favorite spaces to organize. Anyone else? Decluttering this space is a straightforward task, and it can make a huge impact on the overall efficiency of your cleaning routine. Most of us tend to build up a collection of cleaning products here, so it is important to remove those that you don't use in the kitchen. By moving cleaning products that are specific to the bathroom or laundry into their respective spaces, you will free up the kitchen cabinet. Then, your cleaning routine will flow more efficiently.

Storage suggestions

- Turntables are particularly good for storing cleaning products under the sink. Different bottles will not be lined up one behind the other, and you won't have to dig deep to find the one you need.

- Stackable drawers are perfect for storing items such as trash bags and rubber gloves. They come in an array of sizes to allow you to maximize both the depth and height of your space.

- Kitchens often have plumbing around or under the sink. A corner shelf can provide additional storage in difficult spaces.

- Adjustable under-sink organizers are also great if you have lots of pipes to contend with, because they can fit around the pipes and create storage options in the most challenging of spaces.

Kitchen folds

Dish towels

1. Lay the dish towel flat.

2. Fold it in half, left over right. Fold again, from right to left.

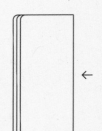

3. Fold down the top.

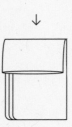

4. Fold up the bottom, and tuck it into the opening. Ready to put away.

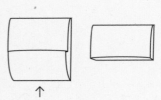

Top tip
As with all my tuck folds, flatten down the inside fold to ensure it isn't creased. If you need to make the fold bigger, simply pull out the sides.

Aprons

1. Lay the apron flat, with the front facing down.

2. Fold down the top, and fold in the loose apron strings.

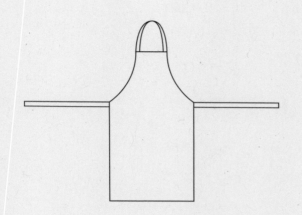

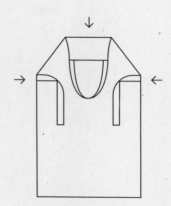

3. Fold in the right side, and then the left.

4. Fold up the bottom, and fold down the top.

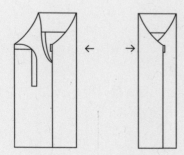

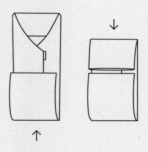

5. Fold up the bottom again, and tuck in the final fold. Ready to put away.

Round tablecloths

1. Fold the tablecloth in half.

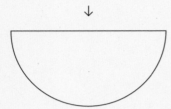

2. Fold in the left side, and then the right.

3. Fold the right side over the left leaving a gap. This fold determines the width of the final product.

4. Fold down the top. This fold will determine the height of the final product.

5. Fold up from the bottom, and tuck in the final fold. Ready to put away.

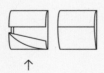

Cleaning cloths

1. Lay the cloth flat, and fold in the left side.

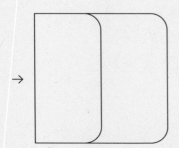

2. Fold over the right side.

3. Fold down from the top.

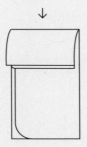

4. Fold up from the bottom, and tuck in the final fold. Ready to put away.

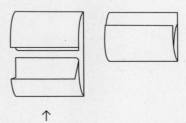

Q&A

"How can I maximize my kitchen storage space?"

- Adjust your shelving to ensure you are not wasting any space between shelves.

- If you can't adjust your shelves, use stackable containers to maximize the height of the space. Or, use under-shelf storage, which does the same job.

- Shelf risers are also a great way to maximize the height in a space.

- Add pull-out shelves to the pantry.

- Use hooks, racks, and extra shelves on the inside of your cabinets to store things like spices, cutting boards, and cleaning cloths.

- Install racks or rods to hang pots and pans.

- Remove low, deep shelving in the pantry, and insert a chest of drawers for a more practical storage option.

- Add shelves for recipe books, or to display serving bowls and so on. As with any open storage, remember you will have to clean and tidy this space regularly.

- When it is time to replace a kitchen item, choose something that is multifunctional. There are many products available, including fruit and vegetable choppers that not only cut but also store the produce, tongs that also whisk (these fold flat so are great for saving space), and scrubbing brushes that dispense soap.

- Explore kitchen gadgets that are specifically designed to save space, such as collapsible measuring cups, strainers, and so on.

- If you have limited counter space, store appliances that are not used regularly elsewhere.

- Respect your boundaries. Not everyone has the space to buy in bulk and store excess stock.

- If space is very limited, look at every blank area in the room: your walls, sides of cabinets, the insides of doors. Add shelves or organizers in these areas if you can.

"How do you stop containers sliding around in the cabinet or on the shelf?"

- Drawer liners are great. You could also add museum gel or clear bumpers to each corner of your container, which will hold it in place, and won't mark the bottom of the cupboard or shelf.

Top tip
Add clear bumpers to each back corner of a picture frame to prevent it from moving on the wall.

Play area

Whether you have a designated playroom, or you store children's toys in another space, mess is inevitable. Embrace it! Toys are there to be played with.

Your goal when organizing toys is to create a practical space. You want somewhere the children can be themselves, access and enjoy their toys, and feel inspired. But it also has to be easy to tidy! To create an effective space, implement systems that are both accessible and enjoyable for children. This will encourage them to participate in the tidying process and have fun doing it.

After decluttering the toys, you may still have more than can fit in your storage. One way to solve this is to use a rotation system. Box up half the toys, and let your children play with the rest. When they become disinterested, swap them for the boxed toys.

Top tip

Toys end up all over the house. Each of my boys has a collapsible basket that we take out each night, and they race to fill theirs the fastest. We transfer the contents of their baskets into their cube storage. It's a final mad hour before winding down for bed, when the kids can release a last burst of energy. It's chaotic but fun, and it makes cleaning up a breeze!

Storage suggestions

To showcase artwork, I have put up a clothesline underneath some shelves, using self-adhesive hooks and some string.

Once the line is full, my boys choose which pieces to remove before adding new ones.

The artwork that has been taken down is then repurposed to wrap presents for their birthdays.

If toys are stored in the living area, choose containers that have lids. That way, when you want to unwind in the evening, the toys are out of sight.

Also, for living room toy storage, explore the potential of your existing furniture. For example, you might be able to use containers with wheels and slide them under the couch. Some pouffes and ottomans also have storage space, which could be used for toys.

Use wall space
to hang nets for
balls and soft toys,
or create a cozy
reading nook with
some hanging shelves.

Toy chests are great for large items, but small
items will get lost at the bottom. Contain
smaller toys and puzzles in zip-seal bags.
I reuse the ones you get with some linen sets.
When you leave the house, you can grab
one of these pouches to put in your bag.

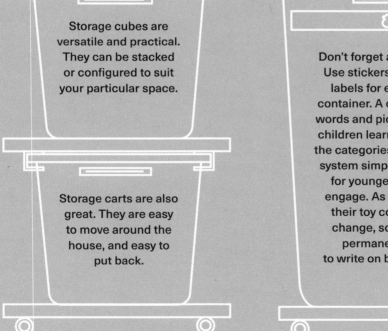

Storage cubes are
versatile and practical.
They can be stacked
or configured to suit
your particular space.

Storage carts are also
great. They are easy
to move around the
house, and easy to
put back.

Don't forget about labeling.
Use stickers to create fun
labels for each storage
container. A combination of
words and pictures can help
children learn to read. Keep
the categories broad and the
system simple, so it is easy
for younger children to
engage. As kids grow up,
their toy collection will
change, so don't use a
permanent marker
to write on boxes directly.

Q&A

"What can younger kids do to help around the home?"

I encourage my boys to get involved in all housework. They both like to restock the toilet paper, Joey loves to practice shooting hoops by throwing dryer balls into the dryer, while Benji spends a lot of time with his dad in the kitchen, cooking and reading the labels on the containers. My boys are young, and I would never force them to do anything. But I encourage them to show appreciation for what they have, and to not take things for granted. I want them to respect their belongings, and part of that means tidying up their toys and helping around the home.

I have worked with many families over the years, and have put together a list of suitable jobs by age. All children are different, so you can customize it to suit your own family.

The tiny tidiers:
Under 5

- Refill the toilet paper holder
- Replenish toilet paper storage
- Lay place mats for dinner
- Sort laundry into piles, by color or type (my boys love finding and pairing all the socks)
- Put dirty clothes into laundry baskets
- Pick up toys
- Collect the mail
- Help fold some items

The clean-up crew:
Ages 5 to 10

- Help put away groceries
- Set the table
- Help prepare meals
- Help fold laundry
- Make their own bed in the morning (it doesn't have to be perfect)
- Put trash and recycling in the outside bin
- Sweep outside
- Weed the garden
- Water the plants

The chore champions:
Age 11 plus

- Vacuum
- Clean car
- Load and turn on washing machine
- Change bed sheets
- Take out trash bins on collection day

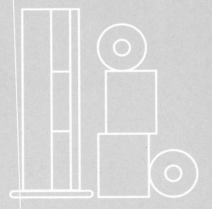

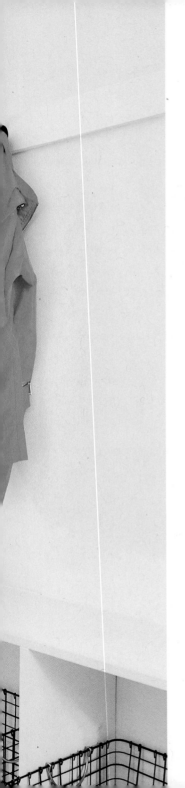

Hallway

As soon as you walk in the front door, what happens? Are shoes kicked off and left where they land? Do the kids throw their bags on the rug? Do you pick up the mail and put it on a shelf or table, to be dealt with another day? It is these initial actions that will determine the type of storage you need in your hallway.

After assessing how you use your space and then decluttering, you will need to tailor your hallway to your specific requirements and preferences. Customize the storage solutions and layout based on the available space.

Storage suggestions

- Use hooks or a rack for hanging jackets, coats, and bags.

- Install a shoe cabinet, or place a shoe rack under a hallway table.

- Assign individual storage to each family member (cube storage is great for the hallway). Make sure that boundaries are clear and that each area is labeled clearly, to ensure items are returned to the correct place.

- If space allows, add a bench or seating area. It will provide a convenient spot for putting on and taking off shoes. Look for benches with built-in storage for added functionality.

- A decorative bowl or a small table with drawers can be used as a catch-all for keys, mail, and other small items.

- Make use of wall space by installing hooks, pegboards, or hanging organizers for additional storage. This can be useful for hats, scarves, flat shoes, or umbrellas.

- Choose decorative storage pieces that combine functionality with aesthetic appeal, such as attractive baskets, boxes, and bins, or floating shelves.

- Store dog leashes on a self-adhesive hook by the door.

- Repurpose vintage crates or trunks. These not only add a rustic touch to a space but also provide sturdy, functional storage for items like shoes and school bags.

- Add a stair basket to collect all the random bits throughout the day. This will make each trip upstairs more productive.

HALLWAY

Maintaining

In The Basics, we discussed
labeling and the importance
of using broad categories. One
thing to note is that I tend not to
label items until two weeks after
I have organized a space. This is
because I want to ensure that
the systems I have created are
working, and that they are easy
to maintain. With that in mind,
let's move on to maintenance.
These are the steps I encourage
you to take so you can enjoy a
newly organized space for
many years to come.

Maintenance plan

Like many things in life—your car, your health, your finances—your home needs maintenance. All the topics we have discussed so far are designed to make this easier:

- Keep things close to where you use them

- Forget the complex systems

- Less is more

- Label in broad categories

- Set boundaries

- Have a game plan

If you follow my suggestions, maintaining your spaces will be a more straightforward task.

Remember:

Function before form, with ease of maintenance the primary goal

About two weeks after you have finished decluttering, organizing, and folding, check how each space is working for you. Is everything as effortless as you would like it to be? Are items easy to see, access, and put back? Are you sticking to your boundaries, or do you need to adjust them?

Once you are sure that everything is working effectively in your space, it is time to integrate daily maintenance and regular checkups into your routine.

Daily maintenance refers to the small tasks we can do to prevent clutter accumulating around the home: removing coffee cups from the bedroom, wiping down the kitchen counters, putting items back where they belong, and so on. Each room should take 5 to 10 minutes a day.

Regular checkups are more detailed but equally important. Circumstances, situations, and people constantly evolve. Perhaps you used to do a particular activity in a space, but now don't. Similarly, your essential items may change over time. Check each space, and remove items that are no longer essential to you in that space—to make room for anything that is.

I have put together a little plan to help.

MAINTENANCE PLAN

Bedroom

Daily maintenance
Make the bed, take cups and dishes back to the kitchen, put away clothes and shoes, and keep surfaces as clear as possible. Keep an eye on the clutter hot spots (chair, bed, flat surfaces), and put away items that don't belong there.

Regular checkups
It is natural for us to accumulate clothing and accessories over time. We forget about the boundaries that we put in place, and things start to slide. To stop your bedroom becoming a mess, schedule a mini declutter and sort-out twice a year. A perfect time to do this is when the seasons change, and you are rotating seasonal wear. Throw away, pass on, or store items that are no longer essential to you. If there is a certain area of the bedroom that tends to attract clutter, fill it with a decorative piece—plant, candle, cushion—to prevent it from being used as a dumping ground. Assess whether additional storage is required.

Night table

Daily maintenance
Keep the surface of your night table clear, and remove anything that doesn't belong there.

Regular checkups
Twice a year, spend about 15 minutes decluttering your night table. Only keep the items that are essential to you in this space.

Baby and children's clothes

Daily maintenance
It would be great if your children could help you out here.
Encourage them to put their dirty clothes in the laundry basket,
and perhaps put away clean clothes if they are old enough.
Nothing has to be perfect, as long as they are trying.

Regular checkups
When you have growing children, you will need to check their
wardrobe and drawers frequently. Remove items that are
damaged or garments they have outgrown. If you wish to pass
on clothes to younger siblings, store them in vacuum bags.
Label the bags clearly (I suggest by age), and ideally move
them into the sibling's storage space.

Laundry

Daily maintenance
Stay on top of the laundry by doing it as soon as you have a full
load. That way, you won't have to do a mountain of laundry over
the weekend. Clean any detergent spillages, put away the clean
laundry as soon as it is dry, and clear the countertops. Before I
had children, laundry was done as and when it was needed. Since
having a family, I have found that doing a load a day really helps
to keep those piles at bay.

Regular checkups
Twice a year, spend an hour decluttering your laundry space.
Get rid of any odd socks that are still hanging on your line
(see page 108). Discard products that you no longer use or that
have expired.

Bathroom

Daily maintenance
Keep the counter space clear, recycle any empty bottles or containers, and put the empty toilet paper roll in the recycling bin. Spot-clean any area that needs it.

Regular checkups
Twice a year, schedule an hour to sort through your makeup, toiletries, and medication. Check all the expiration dates, and perform a mini declutter. Clear out items that you no longer use or that are not essential to you in the space. If you want to establish a new routine in the bathroom, set up a new activity zone and keep any associated items there.

Kitchen

Daily maintenance
Wipe down surfaces, do the dishes, or load the dishwasher. Get into the habit of putting things away immediately after you have used them. Clean as you go.

Regular checkups
Declutter and organize your kitchen twice a year. Check expiration dates on spices and food; inspect your everyday plates, bowls, cups, and glasses for cracks and chips. Throw away, pass on, or store items that are no longer essential to you.

Play area

Daily maintenance

Get the kids involved with everyday tidying up. Put on some music, and make it playful. Encouraging children to help—no matter how small the job—creates healthy habits, and recognizing and rewarding their involvement is paramount to keeping them going. A chore is only a chore if you define it as one.

Regular checkups

Children grow so fast it is scary. Do a mini declutter before birthdays and Christmas, because it is likely an influx of toys will invade the play area. As your children outgrow their toys, donate those that are in good condition, and discard the ones that are broken or have missing pieces.

Hallway

Daily maintenance

Put shoes, bags, and coats back where they belong. Keep the hallway free of clutter, so it feels like a welcoming space when you arrive home. Daily maintenance will really help to keep on top of this often troublesome space.

Regular checkups

Once a year, schedule an hour or two to check the activities that take place in the hallway. You may need to accommodate new items such as backpacks, a stroller, or a dog leash.

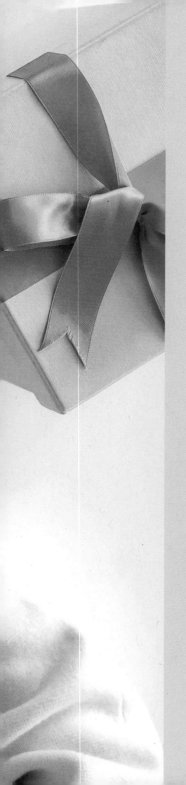

Gift wrapping

There are many traditions that involve exchanging gifts to celebrate different occasions and milestones. While the act of giving a gift is always significant, the way in which it is presented can make it more special.

Creating beautiful gift wraps is a form of art about which I am truly passionate. It serves as my creative outlet, and it allows me to escape the hustle and bustle of daily life.

I am very grateful to have the opportunity to gift wrap for many domestic and international brands, so let's take a peek inside my gift wrapping kit to create your own gift wrap magic.

Gift wrapping kit

- Two pairs of scissors, one pair for paper and one for ribbon. This ensures your ribbon scissors remain sharp to give beautiful, clean cuts.

- Wrapping paper and tissue paper

- Ribbon

- Double-sided tape

- Clear tape

- Pencil

- Single hole punch

- Cards and tags

- Embellishments, such as trinkets, dried flowers, and bells, all of which you can tie onto a gift with ribbon. Secondhand stores often have an array of knick-knacks that are perfect for this.

- Fabric for bottles and other awkwardly shaped gifts

pencil

dried flowers

clear tape

tags

wrapping paper

ribbon

single hole punch

scissors for paper

scissors for ribbon

Viral gift wrapping techniques

Wrapping without tape

This technique requires more paper than traditional wrapping, so is good to use if the recipient reuses paper, if you are using recycled paper, or when you are at the end of a roll.

Measuring

1. Measure the front, side, back, side again, then front of the gift and cut the paper.

2. Create a square by folding up the bottom left corner to the opposite edge, and cut.

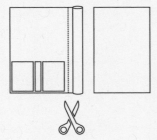

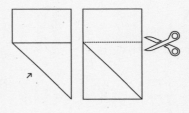

3. Turn your paper on the diagonal, place the gift in the center of the paper, and fold the top corner down over the gift. (You need to have enough paper to cover the gift completely to get the perfect wrap.)

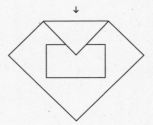

Wrapping

1. Bring the corner closest to you up over the gift, and tuck any excess paper under the top side.

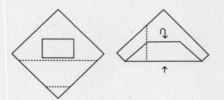

2. Gently push the paper in, and fold it up over the side of the gift toward the center. Repeat on the other side.

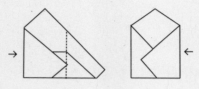

3. Fold the gift over, guiding the paper so the edges remain aligned. Take your time.

4. Tuck in the remaining triangle of paper.

5. This technique also leaves a handy pocket, where you can slot a card.

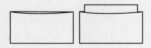

Pocket wrap

Measuring

1. Place the gift on the paper, and make sure the paper will completely cover the gift when you fold it in.

2. To determine the length of the paper, place the gift standing up at the edge of the paper. Lay it on its back, and then tip it onto its opposite end (it is now upside-down). This measurement will give you enough paper to wrap the top and bottom of the gift.

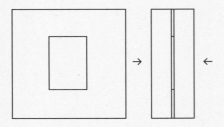

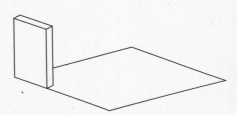

3. Because we are going to create a pocket for a card, we need to increase the length of the paper. Place the card at the top of the gift, and measure the paper so it covers two-thirds the length of the card.

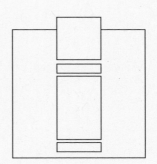

Wrapping

1. Pinch the paper about a third of the way up from the bottom. Fold it upward, making sure you leave enough paper to wrap the ends of your gift. Place the gift face down and upside-down on top of the fold.

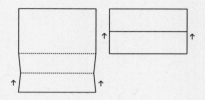

2. Fold in each side over the gift, and seal the join.

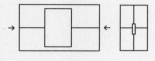

3. Lift up the gift, and fold in the short edges.

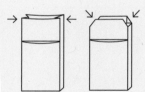

4. Complete the wrap by folding in the long edges, one over the other.

5. Turn over the gift, and place your card inside the pocket you have created.

6. Decorate your gift with a floral embellishment or ribbon.

Bottle wrap

I prefer to use fabric to wrap bottles and other awkwardly shaped gifts.

1. Lay the bottle down in the middle of the fabric.

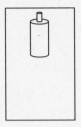

2. Fold up the fabric from the bottom, over the bottle to the top.

3. Take the left-hand corner and push it in toward the side of the bottle. Repeat on the other side.

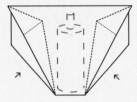

4. You will be left with two triangular shapes, on the bottom and top layers of the fabric.

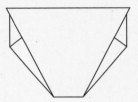

5. Take the top left triangle of fabric, and fold it over the bottle.

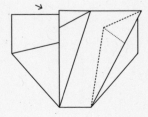

6. Fold the top right triangle over the bottle.

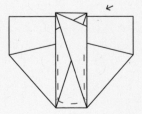

7. Fold the bottom left triangle around the bottle.

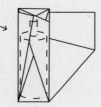

8. Followed by the bottom right triangle.

9. Secure the gift wrap with ribbon at the neck of the bottle.

10. Add embellishments if you wish.

Cylindrical gifts

Measuring

1. Take some ribbon, and wrap it around the item to measure its circumference. I always add about 1 in (2 cm) extra, so I can fold in the edge of the paper.

2. To measure the length of paper needed to cover the top and bottom of the gift, use the ribbon to measure from just over the center of the top of the gift, down the gift, to just past the center of the bottom.

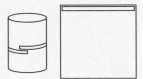

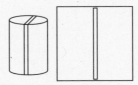

Wrapping

1. To create a crisp, neat finish, fold over the edge of the paper before you start. I attach double-sided tape at this point, so it is ready to stick down.

2. Wrap the paper around the gift, and seal.

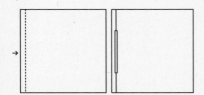

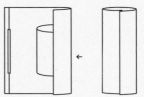

Top tip

There are two ways to wrap the ends of a circular gift. If it is a small item, such as a candle, keep the gift on its side (see right). For a larger item, like a tin of chocolates, gently fold in the bottom in three sections, and work on the top first. Then turn the gift over, and work on the bottom.

3. Fold the inside seam of the paper into the center of the gift. Each fold that you perform after this needs to meet this central spot.

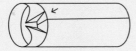

4. Gently pleat the paper, and bring it into the center. Continue to do this until you are at the final pleat.

5. The final pleat will be rectangular in shape, and you should be left with some excess paper that you need to trim.

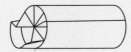

6. Fasten the rectangular pleat.

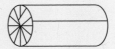

7. Repeat the pleating process on the other end of the gift. Once you master this technique, you can make the pleats smaller, which will, in turn, make the end rectangle smaller.

VIRAL GIFT WRAPPING TECHNIQUES

DIY envelope

1. Start with a square piece of paper 8½x8½ in (22x22 cm). Make two folds of the same size, on the left and right.

2. Open out these folds, and make another fold along the bottom, the same size as the two side folds. Leave this one folded.

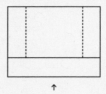

3. Starting with the bottom left corner, and using the first fold you created, fold in the corner to make a triangle.

4. Repeat on the other side.

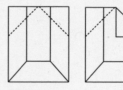

5. Fold in the sides.

6. At the top, use the center of the paper as a marking point, and fold in one corner to create the top of the envelope.

7. Repeat on the other side.

8. Fold over the top section, and tuck in the point. Ready to use.

Q&A

"Where do you store gift wrapping items?"

I store all of my wrapping tools and materials in a chest of drawers. Rolls of paper are placed in their own drawer, and I use a combination of drawer dividers and drawer inserts for smaller things, such as tapes, ribbons, and decorative items. Here are some alternative storage ideas:

- A gift wrapping storage bag is an easy way to keep your paper and accessories contained and organized.

- Get creative and build your own gift wrapping station. Attach a pegboard organizer to the back of a door, and use containers to store tapes, scissors, and other gift wrapping essentials.

- Use tension rods in a small cabinet or closet to store paper.

- Use adhesive hooks and wooden dowels to display paper on the wall. Place a rolling cart underneath, and store your other gift wrapping supplies there.

Index

Picture Credits

Acknowledgments

To you, my reader, thank you. I hope that you have enjoyed this book and that it encourages you to organize for yourself and nobody else. It is all about you.

To my wonderful agent Oscar, who I have the utmost respect and gratitude for. You have given me the confidence to keep going and the strength to keep pushing. "Thank you" just doesn't seem enough.

To Cara, Sophie, Jordan, and Becky, the incredible team at DK I am so lucky to work with: thank you for all your help, support, and guidance. You have made a dream come true, and I will be forever thankful.

Craig and Brad, it wouldn't have been possible to write this book without taking a short sabbatical from work. Thank you for granting me this. You have both always believed in me, and I appreciate you both tremendously. You are amazing.

A special thank you to Wardy, Lou, and Mel for the love and laughter, and for always leaving the key out.

For your ongoing, unwavering support, Kevin and Heidi—thank you. You are a constant source of inspiration. Who knows where I would be without you both.

To my family and the fabulous Lynches—Dad, Alan, Jason, Richard, Gary, Sally, Liam, Lisa, Grania, Joe, and Keith—thank you for being my biggest supporters and for getting so excited about all things Effective Spaces. Mum, you are my greatest influence and motivator; this is for you.

And finally, to Gavin, Joey, and Benji—we did it and this is just the beginning for us.

I love you. xx

Penguin Random House

DK LONDON
Editorial Director Cara Armstrong
Senior Editor Sophie Blackman
Senior US Editor Megan Douglass
Designer Jordan Lambley
Senior Production Editor Tony Phipps
Senior Production Controller Luca Bazzoli
Sales Material & Jackets Co-ordinator Emily Cannings
Jacket Designer Jordan Lambley
Editorial Manager Ruth O'Rourke
Art Director Maxine Pedliham
Publishing Director Katie Cowan

Design Evi-O
Illustration Evi-O | Katherine Zhang, Siena Zadro
Editorial Becky Gee

First American Edition, 2024
Published in the United States by DK Publishing,
a division of Penguin Random House LLC
1745 Broadway, 20th Floor, New York, NY 10019

24 25 26 27 28 10 9 8 7 6 5 4 3
004-340124-Apr/2024

A catalog record for this book
is available from the Library of Congress.
ISBN 978-0-7440-9515-9

DK books are available at special discounts when purchased in bulk
for sales promotions, premiums, fund-raising, or educational use.
For details, contact: DK Publishing Special Markets,
1745 Broadway, 20th Floor, New York, NY 10019
SpecialSales@dk.com

Printed and bound in Canada

www.dk.com

MIX
Paper | Supporting
responsible forestry
FSC™ C018179

This book was made with Forest
Stewardship Council™ certified
paper—one small step in DK's
commitment to a sustainable future.
Learn more at **www.dk.com/uk/
information/sustainability**